Mass Confusion

JAMES AKIN

Mass Confusion

The Do's and Don'ts of Catholic Worship

Second Expanded Edition

CATHOLIC ANSWERS
SAN DIEGO
1999

Published by Catholic Answers, Inc.
P.O. Box 17490
San Diego, California 92177
(888) 291–8000 (orders)
(619) 541–1154 (fax)
www.catholic.com (web)

Cover design by Tammi Shore/Shore Design Associates
Printed in the United States of America
ISBN 1–888992–05–0

Contents

Abbreviations

AAS   *Acta Apostolicae Sedis*

AGI   U.S. Bishops, "Appendix to the General Instruction for the Dioceses of the United States." Citations taken from *The Sacramentary* (Collegeville: Liturgical Press, 1985)

BCL   Bishops' Committee on Liturgy

CB   *Ceremonial of Bishops* (Collegeville, Minnesota: Liturgical Press, 1990)

CCC   *Catechism of the Catholic Church* (San Francisco: Ignatius Press, 1994)

CCEO   *Codex Canonum Ecclesiarum Orientalum—Code of Canons of the Eastern Churches* (Washington: Canon Law Society of America, 1992)

CDS   Congregation for the Discipline of the Sacraments

CMRR   *Ceremonies of the Modern Roman Rite* (San Francisco: Ignatius, 1995)

CSDW   Congregation for the Sacraments and Divine Worship

CDW   Congregation for Divine Worship

CIC   *Codex Iuris Canonici—Code of Canon Law* (Washington: Canon Law Society of America, 1983)

D   Denzinger's *Enchiridion Symbolorum*

DC   John Paul II, *Dominicae Cenae* ("On the Mystery and Worship of the Eucharist"), February 24, 1980

DMC   "Directory for Masses with Children." Citations taken from *The Sacramentary* (Collegeville, Minnesota: Liturgical Press, 1985)

DOL   *Documents on the Liturgy* (Collegeville, Minnesota: Liturgical Press, 1983)

DS   Denzinger and Schönmetzer, *Enchiridion Symbolorum*, 36th ed. (Barcelona: Herder, 1976)

FC   CDS, *Fidei Custos*, 30 April 1969 (citations taken from DOL)

GIRM   "General Instruction of the Roman Missal." Citations taken from *The Sacramentary* (Collegeville, Minnesota: Liturgical Press, 1985)

HLS   U.S. Bishops, "This Holy and Living Sacrifice: Directory for the Celebration and Reception of Communion under Both Kinds" (citations taken from LD)

IC   CDS, *Immensae Caritatis* (citations taken from DOL)

ICP   *Instruction on Certain Questions Regarding the Collaboration of the Non-Ordained Faithful in the Sacred Ministry of Priest,* issued by the Congregation for the Clergy *et al.* (Libreria Editrice Vaticana translation)

ID   CSDW, *Inaestimabile Donum*

LD   *The Liturgy Documents: A Parish Resource*, 3rd ed. (Chicago: Liturgy Training Publications, 1991)

LFM   *Lectionary for Mass for Use in the Dioceses of the United States of America*

NCCB   National Conference of Catholic Bishops

PS   CDW, *Paschales Solemnitatis* ("Preparation and Celebration of the Easter Feasts")

SC   Vatican II, *Sacrosanctum Concilium* (citations taken from LD)

VC2   Austin Flannery, O.P., gen. ed., *Vatican Council II: The Conciliar and Post Conciliar Documents*, vol. 1 (Boston: St. Paul Books and Media, 1992)

Introduction

This work is intended as a guide to the Church's law concerning the proper way to celebrate the liturgy. It also attempts to answer some of the most commonly asked questions about what are and are not liturgical abuses.

This book can cover the state of liturgical affairs only at the time of its current edition. The regulations recorded here are those in force at the time of the publication. Changes in the Church's liturgical law will be reflected in future editions.

Because liturgical abuses cause such controversy in the Church, I should point out that the intention of this book is to describe what the liturgical law of the Church *is*, not my opinions on what the liturgical law of the Church *should be*.

I do not pretend to be an expert in liturgical law. However, as is so often pointed out, the liturgy is not the exclusive domain of liturgical "experts." It belongs to the whole people of God. Even the most humble person has the right to study and inform himself of what constitutes authentic Catholic liturgy and to compare it with the liturgies he experiences, making his voice heard among the people of God when something inauthentic is found.

I would also like to express my profound thanks to the experts who reviewed drafts of the manuscript to help ensure accuracy and completeness, especially the Very Rev. Peter M. J. Stravinskas, Ph.D., S.T.D., of Newman House in Mt. Pocono, Pennsylvania; Edward Peters, J.D., J.C.D., of San Diego; and, from the St. Joseph Foundation in San Antonio, Texas, Charles Wilson, M.T.S. (executive director), Lou Dellert, M.T.S. (vice president/case administrator), Duane Galles, J.D., J.C.L. (vice president for canonical affairs), and Rev. James R. P. O'Connor, S.T.L., Mag. Theo., J.C.L. (canonical consultant). Any defects that remain are present in spite of their thorough and accurate efforts.

JAMES AKIN
November 4, 1997
Memorial of St. Charles Borromeo

1. The Liturgy

What Is the Liturgy?

The *Catechism of the Catholic Church* explains liturgy this way:

> The word "liturgy" originally meant a "public work" or a "service in the name of/on behalf of the people." In Christian tradition it means the participation of the People of God in "the work of God" (cf. John 17:4). Through the liturgy Christ, our Redeemer and High Priest, continues the work of our redemption in, with, and through his Church.
>
> In the New Testament the word "liturgy" refers not only to the celebration of divine worship but also to the proclamation of the Gospel and to active charity (cf. Luke 1:23; Acts 13:2; Rom. 15:16, 27; 2 Cor. 9:12; Phil. 2:14–17, 25, 30). In all of these situations it is a question of the service of God and neighbor. In a liturgical celebration the Church is servant in the image of her Lord, the one "leitourgos" (cf. Hebrews 8:2, 6); she shares in Christ's priesthood (worship), which is both prophetic (proclamation) and kingly (service of charity) [CCC 1069–1070].

This theological explanation of liturgy is given a concrete form in the current *Code of Canon Law* (1983):

Canon 834

§1. The Church fulfills its office of sanctifying in a special way in the sacred liturgy, which is indeed the exercise of the priestly office of Jesus Christ; in it [the liturgy] through sensible signs the sanctification of humankind is signified and effected in a manner proper to each of the signs and the whole of the public worship of God is carried on by the mystical Body of Jesus Christ, that is, by the Head and the members.

§2. This worship takes place when it is carried out in the name of the Church by persons lawfully deputed and through acts approved by the authority of the Church.

To synthesize these statements, one might say that the liturgy is the public worship of the Church, carried out in the name of the Church by those authorized to conduct or participate in it. Public, in this case, does not indicate the presence of many people. Even a Mass with only one person present besides the celebrant counts as a public act of worship.

Pope John Paul II has also reminded us:

> Every priest who offers the holy Sacrifice should recall that during this Sacrifice it is not only he with his community that is praying but the whole Church, which is thus expressing in this sacrament her spiritual unity, among other ways by the use of the approved liturgical text [DC 12].

There are many different forms of liturgy that the Church uses in its worship of God. The most common of these are the celebration of the sacraments and the Liturgy of the Hours, which is the Church's cycle of daily prayer. Also included are many blessings and sacramentals.

Of all liturgies, the Mass is the most important. The *General Instruction of the Roman Missal* states:

> The celebration of Mass, the action of Christ and the people of God arrayed hierarchically, is for the universal and the local Church, as well as for each person, the center of the whole Christian life. In the Mass we have the high point of the work that in Christ, his Son, we offer to the Father. During the cycle of the year, moreover, the mysteries of redemption are recalled in the Mass in such a way that they are somehow made present. All other liturgical rites and all other works of the Christian life

are linked with the Eucharistic celebration, flow from it, and have it as their end [GIRM 1].

Because of the preeminence of the Mass in the Church's liturgical life, and because it is the liturgy that the faithful experience most often, the present work will focus on the Mass, its proper celebration, and liturgical abuses that often occur in its context.

Since the Mass is the supreme form of liturgy on earth, it is important that all play their proper roles. The *General Instruction* stresses:

> [I]t is of the greatest importance that the celebration of the Mass, the Lord's Supper, be so arranged that the ministers and the faithful who take their own proper part in it may more fully receive its good effects. This is the reason why Christ the Lord instituted the Eucharistic sacrifice of his Body and Blood and entrusted it to the Church, his beloved Bride, as the memorial of his passion and resurrection [GIRM 2].

Unfortunately, in recent years many have *not* played their proper roles but have deviated from them, to the harm of the faithful and the Church and its mission.

Recent Liturgical History

By the time of the Second Vatican Council (1962–1965), a liturgical reform movement had been growing in the Church for over a century, encouraged by wise and holy pontiffs such as Pius X and Pius XII.

When the Council met, it embraced this movement and mandated that several particular reforms be made after the Council. Among these were a simplification of the prayers used in the Mass of the Latin Rite (SC 50) and a greater but still limited use of vernacular languages in addition to Latin (SC 36, 54), with allowances for certain local reforms subject to approval by the Holy See (SC 40).

Latin had been the official language of Latin Rite Catholic churches since the early centuries, and in the 1500s the Council of Trent reaffirmed the use of Latin as a liturgical language. The *General Instruction of the Roman Missal* remarks:

> The Council of Trent recognized the great catechetical value of the celebration of Mass. . . . Many were pressing for permission to use the vernacular in celebrations of the Eucharistic sacrifice, but the Council, judging the conditions of that age, felt bound to answer such a request with a reaffirmation of the Church's traditional teaching. This teaching is that the Eucharistic sacrifice is, first and foremost, the action of Christ himself and therefore the manner in which the faithful take part in the Mass does not affect the efficacy belonging to it. The Council thus stated in firm but measured words: "Although the Mass contains much instruction for the faithful, it did not seem expedient to the Fathers that as a general rule it be celebrated in the vernacular" (Trent, session 22, *Doctrine on the Holy Sacrifice of the Mass* 8). The Council accordingly anathematized [excommunicated] anyone maintaining that "the rite of the Roman Church, in which part of the canon and the words of consecration are spoken in a low voice, should be condemned or that the Mass must be celebrated only in the vernacular" (*ibid.*, canon 9). Although the Council of Trent on the one hand prohibited the use of the vernacular in Mass, nevertheless, on the other, it did direct pastors to substitute appropriate catechesis: "Lest Christ's flock go hungry . . ." (*op. cit.*) [GIRM Introduction, 11].

By the twentieth century, the situation had changed and there was no longer a movement in the Catholic Church denying the validity of liturgical worship conducted in Latin, so the Second Vatican Council revisited the issue:

Convened in order to adapt the Church to the contemporary requirements of its apostolic task, Vatican II examined thoroughly, as had Trent, the pedagogic and pastoral character of the liturgy. Since no Catholic would deny the lawfulness and efficacy of a sacred rite celebrated in Latin, the Council was able to acknowledge that "the use of the mother tongue frequently may be of great advantage to the people" (cf. SC 36) and gave permission for its use [GIRM Introduction, 12].

After the Council, the Holy See received numerous requests from local hierarchies for greater use of the vernacular in their territories. The approval of these requests led to much freer use of the vernacular. Austin Flannery, O.P., explains:

> The Constitution on the Sacred Liturgy had allowed a very restricted use of the vernacular in the Mass . . . but left the way open for an appeal by hierarchies to the Holy See for more radical concessions. . . . The Constitution also allowed ordinaries to grant permission to individual clerics to recite the office in the vernacular if they found it very difficult to recite in Latin. . . . However, restrictions on the use of the vernacular were progressively lifted in the face of representations by hierarchies from all over the world, until by 1971 the use of the vernacular in public Masses was left entirely to the judgment of episcopal conferences, to the judgment of individual priests for private Masses, and of the ordinary for divine office, in private, in common, and in choir [VC2 39].

The numerous requests received by the Holy See for greater local use of the vernacular is even noted in the introduction to the *General Instruction of the Roman Missal*. After the vernacular was more often allowed,

> [t]he enthusiasm in response to this decision was so great that, under the leadership of the bishops and the Apostolic See, it has resulted in the permission for all liturgical celebrations in which the faithful participate to be in the vernacular for the sake of a

better comprehension of the mystery being celebrated [GIRM Introduction, 12].

In conjunction with the change in the language of the liturgy was the revision that the Council mandated for the liturgical texts themselves. This revision culminated in the release of the Missal of 1969. Pope Paul VI, who promulgated the revised Missal, stressed that the Mass itself was the same, only its order had changed:

> [B]e very sure of one point: Nothing of the substance of the traditional Mass has been altered . . . . [T]he Mass in its new order is and will remain the Mass it has been and in some aspects bears increased evidence of being so. The unity between the Lord's Supper, the sacrifice of the cross, and the renewal representing both in the Mass in unfailingly affirmed and celebrated in the new rite, just as it was in the old. The Mass is and will remain the memorial of the Lord's Supper. There, changing bread and wine into his own Body and Blood, he instituted the sacrifice of the New Testament. By virtue of the priesthood conferred on his apostles, he willed that sacrifice to be renewed in its identical reality, but in a different mode, that is, unbloodily and sacramentally, as his perpetual memorial until his final coming. . . .
>
> Do not think that all this is meant to change the true, traditional essence of the Mass. Seek rather to learn to appreciate how the Church, through this new and more explicit language, wishes to give greater effectiveness to its liturgical message, and wishes, in a more direct and pastoral way, to draw near to each one of its children. . . . Let us then not speak of a "new Mass" [Paul VI, *General Audience of Nov. 19, 1969;* DOL 1758–1759].

The change was made, the Pope indicated, for sound pastoral reasons, including a greater role for the liturgy in evangelism and catechetics. For example, now it would be more accessible to groups who could not be expected to know Latin, such as young children and non-Catholics who might be considering the Church (cf. Paul VI, *General Audience of Nov. 26, 1969,* DOL 1760–1764).

At the time, it was also expected that the promulgation of the new, authoritative order of the Mass would put to an end liturgical experiments and abuses that had appeared during the period leading up to and following the Council. The Pope stated:

> This reform puts an end to uncertainty, arguments, and misguided experiments. It summons us back to that uniformity of rites and of attitudes that is proper to the Catholic Church, the heir and continuator of the first Christian community that was "of one heart and of one soul" [Acts 4:32]. The harmonious chorus of its prayer is one of the signs and strengths of the Church's unity and catholicity. The change about to take place must not shatter or disturb that harmony, but rather intensify it and make it resound with a new, rejuvenated spirit [*op. cit.*, no. 8, DOL 1758].

Unfortunately, while there are many positive aspects to the liturgical renewal, the hoped-for end to experiments and abuses has not materialized. In many respects, these experiments and abuses have accelerated and grown more widespread since the promulgation of the revision of the Mass, and the "harmonious chorus" of the Church's liturgy to which Pope Paul VI referred *has* been disturbed and shattered, contrary to his wish.

The problem of unauthorized experiments and abuses has grown so great that today no one attending a Catholic church can be unaware of the difficulties that have appeared in implementing the Church's liturgical reform. Even if they are blessed by having a parish that faithfully and reverently follows the Church's rubrics for the Mass, they cannot help but be scandalized by reports coming to them from friends and relatives who attend other parishes and from accounts in the Catholic press.

Following the promulgation of the revision of the Mass, the problem grew so severe that in 1980 Pope John Paul II issued a letter to the world's bishops in which he stated:

> I would like to ask forgiveness—in my own name and in the name of all of you, venerable and dear brothers in the episcopate—for everything which, for whatever reason, through whatever human weakness, impatience or negligence, and also through the at-times partial, one-sided and erroneous application of the directives of the Second Vatican Council, may have caused scandal and disturbance concerning the interpretation of the doctrine and the veneration due to this great sacrament, [the Holy Eucharist]. And I pray the Lord Jesus that in the future we may avoid in our manner of dealing with this sacred mystery anything which could weaken or disorient in any way the sense of reverence and love that exists in our faithful people [DC 12].

And he added:

> Above all I wish to emphasize that the problems of the liturgy, and in particular of the Eucharistic Liturgy, must not be an occasion for dividing Catholics and for threatening the unity of the Church. This is demanded by an elementary understanding of that sacrament which Christ has left us as the source of spiritual unity. And how could the Eucharist, which in the Church is the *sacramentum pietatis, signum unitatis, vinculum caritatis*, form between us at this time a point of division and a source of distortion of thought and of behavior, instead of being the focal point and constitutive center, which it truly is in its essence, of the unity of the Church herself? [*ibid.*, 13].

That year the Holy Father also authorized the Sacred Congregation for the Sacraments and Divine Worship to issue a document titled *Inaestimabile Donum* or "Instruction Concerning the Worship of the Eucharistic Mystery." (Copies may be obtained in booklet form from Pauline Books and Media, run by the Daughters of St. Paul, and in file form at a variety of locations on the Internet.)

The instruction dealt with many of the liturgical abuses going on in the Church, and in offering an appraisal of the current crisis of liturgical abuses it noted that, while there had been many positive developments due to the implementation of the liturgical reform,

> these encouraging and positive aspects cannot suppress concern at the varied and frequent abuses being reported from different parts of the Catholic world: the confusion of roles, especially regarding the priestly ministry and the role of the laity (indiscriminate shared recitation of the Eucharistic Prayer, homilies given by lay people, lay people distributing Communion while the priests refrain from doing so); an increasing loss of the sense of the sacred (abandonment of liturgical vestments, the Eucharist celebrated outside church without real need, lack of reverence and respect for the Blessed Sacrament, etc.); misunderstanding of the ecclesial character of the Liturgy (the use of private texts, the proliferation of unapproved Eucharistic Prayers, the manipulation of the liturgical texts for social and political ends). In these cases we are face to face with a real falsification of the Catholic liturgy . . .
>
> None of these things can bring good results. The consequences are—and cannot fail to be—the impairing of the unity of faith and worship in the Church, doctrinal uncertainty, scandal and bewilderment among the People of God, and the near inevitability of violent reactions [ID, Introduction].

Regrettably, the directives issued by the Sacred Congregation have not been implemented in many areas, largely because the laity have often been unaware of them and thus have not pointed out or been able to identify and document liturgical abuses when they have occurred.

Although the present work aims to assist with this need, no book of this length can possibly deal with every situation or liturgical abuse. We can only provide information on some of the most commonly reported abuses in our look at the Church's requirements concerning the proper celebration of the liturgy.

The Rights of the Laity

The starting point for understanding liturgical abuses is understanding *why* they are abuses and *whom* they abuse. A liturgical abuse—an instance where the liturgy is conducted out of accord with the Church's liturgical law—is not merely a misuse of dead text on a page in a lectionary or a sacramentary. It is an abuse of a living person, or rather, a *group* of living persons —the faithful who attend the liturgy—and it is an abuse of the sanctity of the Church, which requires its rituals to be performed in a certain way.

This is because the faithful have a *right* to experience the liturgy as the Church has designed and intended it. If those who plan or conduct a liturgy tamper with the Church's design for it, they are abusing the faithful by denying their right to an authentic liturgy.

The Church openly declares the laity's right to a proper liturgy:

> The faithful have a right to a true liturgy, which means the liturgy desired and laid down by the Church, which has in fact indicated where adaptations may be made as called for by pastoral requirements in different places or by different groups of people. Undue experimentation, changes, and creativity bewilder the faithful [ID, Introduction].

This right is guaranteed in the *Code of Canon Law:*

CANON 214

The Christian faithful have the right to worship God according to the prescriptions of their own rite approved by the legitimate pastors of the Church, and to follow their own form of
spiritual life consonant with the teaching of the Church.

A fundamental right and duty of the laity is to permeate the
temporal order with the spirit of the gospel (canon 225 §2).
This right, like the other rights of the faithful, is meant to help
us accomplish our vocation in the Church and to help us gain
eternal life.

The laity cannot accomplish these tasks without access to
the spiritual goods of the Church. Thus canons 214 and 846
(below) are foundational statutes that guarantee the right of
the Christian faithful to worship according to the liturgical
norms established by the competent ecclesiastical authorities.
Canon 846, in particular, imposes upon the sacred ministers
the obligation to conduct public worship, especially the Holy
Sacrifice of the Mass, in keeping with the appropriate liturgical
books.

Who Can Change the Liturgy?

Most liturgical abuses involve the omission of a mandatory
part of the liturgy, the addition to the liturgy of something the
Church has not authorized, or the change of a liturgical text
to say something other than what the Church has authorized.

People in situations where liturgical abuses are occurring
typically wish to know who has the authority to alter the liturgy. Since the liturgy is the public or corporate worship the
Church gives to God, those whom God has given charge of

the Church (cf. 1 Thess. 5:12, Heb. 13:17) have the responsibility of regulating the liturgy to make sure that it is conducted properly.

The way the liturgy is regulated at the present time is spelled out in the *Code of Canon Law:*

CANON 838

§1. The supervision of the sacred liturgy depends solely on the authority of the Church which resides in the Apostolic See and, in accord with the law, the diocesan bishop.

§2. It is for the Apostolic See to order the sacred liturgy of the universal Church, to publish liturgical books, to review their translations into the vernacular languages, and to see that liturgical ordinances are faithfully observed everywhere.

§3. It pertains to the [national] conferences of bishops to prepare translations of the liturgical books into the vernacular languages, with the appropriate adaptations within the limits defined in the liturgical books themselves, and to publish them with the prior review by the Holy See.

§4. It pertains to the diocesan bishop in the church entrusted to him, within the limits of his competence, to issue liturgical norms by which all are bound.

The pattern is for the Holy See to order the liturgy, for the conference of bishops to translate it and adapt it to its own jurisdiction, and for the diocesan bishop to issue additional liturgical norms.

An example of the latter would be what time the Easter Vigil will be celebrated in a particular locale. However, the diocesan bishop may not make norms that conflict with those that have been established by the Holy See. Similarly, the conference of bishops must obtain the confirmation of the Holy See before any translations or adaptations it has proposed are permitted to be used (this is what is meant by "the *prior* review of the Holy See").

This means that no one, whether lector, extraordinary minister of Holy Communion, deacon, priest, bishop, or even a national conference of bishops, is able to authorize changes in the liturgy that conflict with what has been approved by the Holy See. The Holy See must ratify any such changes and adaptations *before* they can be put into practice. Thus the *Code of Canon Law* states:

CANON 846 §1

The liturgical books approved by the competent authority are to be faithfully observed in the celebration of the sacraments; therefore, no one on personal authority may add, remove, or change anything in them.

Inaestimabile Donum also stresses this:

One who offers worship to God on the Church's behalf in a way contrary to that which is laid down by the Church with God-given authority and which is customary in the Church is guilty of falsification.

The use of unauthorized texts means a loss of the necessary connection between the *lex orandi* ["the law of prayer"] and the *lex credendi* ["the law of belief"]. The Second Vatican Council's admonition in this regard must be remembered: "No person, even if he be a priest, may add, remove, or change anything in the Liturgy on his own authority" [SC 22]. And Paul VI of venerable memory stated that: "Anyone who takes advantage of the reform to indulge in arbitrary experiments is wasting energy and offending the ecclesial sense" [ID, Introduction, citing Paul VI, address of August 22, 1973, *L'Osservatore Romano*, August 23, 1973].

Pope John Paul II also stressed:

The priest . . . cannot consider himself a "proprietor" who can make free use of the liturgical text and of the sacred rite as if it were his own property, in such a way as to stamp it with his own arbitrary personal style. At times this latter might seem more effective, and it may better correspond to subjective piety; nevertheless, objectively it is always a betrayal of that union which should find its proper expression in the sacrament of unity.

Every priest who offers the Holy Sacrifice should recall that during this Sacrifice it is not only he with his community that is praying but the whole Church, which is thus expressing in this sacrament her spiritual unity, among other ways by the use of the approved liturgical text. To call this position "mere insistence on uniformity" would only show ignorance of the objective requirements of authentic unity, and would be a symptom of harmful individualism [DC 12].

Church's Liturgical Documents

The weight of a particular liturgical directive varies depending on, among other things, the source in which it is found. Among the most authoritative sources is the current (1983) *Code of Canon Law* (CIC). Normally, anything that the Code says is binding on the Roman Rite of the Catholic Church. However, the Code has little to say about liturgical matters, as it is not principally a book of liturgical law (see canon 2).

We have already cited *Sacrosanctum Concilium* (SC), Vatican II's 1963 constitution on the sacred liturgy, which lays out the essential principles of the liturgical reform as envisioned by Vatican II. However, many things in *Sacrosanctum Concilium* have been supplemented or implemented by post-conciliar legislation.

The primary liturgical resource for the Mass is the *Missale Romanum* ("Roman Missal"), which includes the Lectionary (book of Scripture readings) and the Sacramentary (book containing the prayers of the Mass). Whatever the *Missale Romanum* directs one to do is binding, unless it is modified by other law or by immemorial custom.

Contained in the Sacramentary is a preface known as the *General Instruction of the Roman Missal* (GIRM) which is part of the Church's universal liturgical law and is binding on all Roman Rite celebrations of the liturgy. This preface gives general information about the Mass and how it is to be celebrated.

In sacramentaries for use in America there is also an *Appendix to the General Instruction for the Dioceses of the United States*. It contains approved American adaptations of the *General Instruction*.

The body of the Sacramentary, which contains the texts for the prayers, contains short directions printed in red ink. These are called "rubrics," from the Latin term for "red." As with everything in the *Missale Romanum*, they are binding unless modified by proper Church authority. It is these short directions that we will be referring to when we quote or cite "the rubrics." To find the rubric we are talking about, turn in the Sacramentary to the section of the Mass being discussed.

Copies of the *Code of Canon Law*, the Lectionary, and the Sacramentary may be obtained through any Catholic bookstore. One can also ask to examine them at any local parish, either in the parish library or from a priest. They can also often be obtained at college or university libraries.

In this book we will also quote from several other sources that are less readily available. They can often be found at the diocesan office, in the libraries of Catholic universities, and collected in books of liturgical documents that one can purchase through a Catholic bookstore (see "Where to Go for More Help" in chapter 12).

The first of these is the publication *Acta Apostolicae Sedis* ("Acts of the Apostolic See," AAS), the official commentary in which the Holy See publishes the laws, decrees, and acts of congregations and tribunals in the Roman Curia.

In addition to AAS, we will be quoting from *Notitiae*, the publication of the Holy See's Congregation for Divine Worship and the Discipline of the Sacraments (a fusion of two former bodies, the Congregation for Divine Worship and the Congregation for the Discipline of the Sacraments, which were originally united in 1975, separated in 1984, and united again in 1988). This body has competency for matters pertaining to the liturgy—e.g., granting permission for local adaptations, issuing pronouncements on the Church's liturgical law, etc.

We will also be quoting from several of the congregation's instructions, including *Fidei Custos* (on extraordinary ministers of Holy Communion), *Immensae Caritatis* (dealing with the reception of Communion in certain circumstances), *Paschales Solemnitatis* (dealing with the special celebrations of Holy Week), and especially *Inaestimabile Donum*, which we have already quoted.

Inaestimabile Donum is the Church's 1980 response to the numerous liturgical abuses occurring in the Church. Some parts of it are now outdated, but we will only cite those parts that remain in force. *Inaestimabile Donum* was "prepared by the Sacred Congregation for the Sacraments and Divine Worship, [and] was approved on April 17, 1980, by the Holy Father, John Paul II, who confirmed it with his own authority and ordered it to be published and to be observed by all concerned" (ID, Conclusion).

We will be citing a U.S. bishops' work favorably reviewed by the Holy See in 1984 for use in the United States and titled *This Holy and Living Sacrifice: Directory for the Celebration and Reception of Communion under Both Kinds*.

One final authoritative document was released on November 13, 1997, just as this book was going to press. The document, titled *Instruction on Certain Questions Regarding the Collaboration of the Non-Ordained Faithful in the Sacred Ministry of Priest*, was released by a group of eight dicasteries of the Holy See. The document is intended to answer certain questions and respond to complaints of abuses that the Holy See has received. It states:

> The scope of this present document is simply to provide a clear, authoritative response to the many pressing requests which have come to our Dicasteries from Bishops, Priests and Laity seeking clarification in the light of specific cases of new forms of "pastoral activity" of the non-ordained on both parochial and diocesan levels. . . .
>
> In the light of the aforementioned principles, remedies, based on the normative discipline of the Church, and deemed opportune to correct abuses which have been brought to the attention of our Dicasteries, are hereby set forth [ICP, Premise].

The abuses of which the document speaks are widespread in many areas (including much of the United States), where the laity have been assigned roles that should properly be filled by priests, thus blurring and eroding the necessary distinction between the priesthood and the laity. The instruction states:

> [The tasks of the laity in the Church] are most closely linked to the duties of pastors, (which office requires reception of the sacrament of Orders), it is necessary that all who are in any way involved in this collaboration, exercise particular care to safeguard the nature and mission of sacred ministry and the vocation and secular character of the lay faithful. It must be remembered that "collaboration with" does not, in fact, mean "substitution for" [ICP, Premise].

Signing the document were the presidents, prefects, pro-prefects, and secretaries of eight dicasteries. These were the Congregation for the Clergy, the Pontifical Council for the Laity, the Congregation for the Doctrine of the Faith, the Congregation for Divine Worship and the Discipline of the Sacraments, the Congregation for Bishops, the Congregation for the Evangelization of Peoples, the Congregation for Institutes of

Consecrated Life and Societies of Apostolic Life, and the Pontifical Council for the Interpretation of Legislative Texts. This is an unprecedented number of curial offices signing a text that is being issued, and it underscores the seriousness with which the Holy See intends the text to be taken.

The authority of the text as a legislative document is established in its conclusion, which states:

> All particular laws, customs, and faculties conceded by the Holy See *ad experimentum* ["to experiment"] or other ecclesiastical authorities which are contrary to the foregoing norms are hereby revoked.
>
> *The Supreme Pontiff, in Audience of the 13th of August 1997 approved* in forma specifica *this present Instruction and ordered its promulgation* [ICP, Conclusion].

The statement that the Supreme Pontiff approved the document *in forma specifica* ("in its specific form") means that its norms have the same force of law as if the Roman Pontiff had issued them directly.

The declaration that "[a]ll prior laws, customs, and faculties . . . which are contrary to the foregoing norms are hereby revoked" creates a clean slate, legislatively. It does not matter who may have issued a norm—offices or individuals in the Holy See, the national conference of bishops, the local bishop, or the parish priest. *All* previous policies contrary to the document's norms, no matter who issued or ostensibly issued them, have been revoked by the authority of the Supreme Pontiff. In one fell swoop, this removes any pretense of legitimacy to contrary practices. It does not matter what anyone has said in the past. The pope's approval of the text *in forma specifica* means that the document's directives unambiguously are the Church's *law*.

At the time of this writing, pamphlet versions of the instruction have not yet been published in the United States. However, the document is available on the Holy See's web site at www.vatican.va.

Mention should be made of one document that does *not* have canonical authority. It is called *Environment and Art in Catholic Worship*. This document is part of a class of documents issued by the U.S. Bishops' Committee on the Liturgy that does not have binding authority, for one reason, because they have not been approved by the National Council of Catholic Bishops or the Holy See.

Environment and Art in Catholic Worship (EACW) is frequently used as a basis for major, austere, and often aesthetically displeasing renovations in parishes. When parishioners question these proposed changes, they are often told—*incorrectly*—that EACW is the Church's liturgical law and that the U.S. bishops approved it. The bishops didn't. EACW is the publication of a single committee and is not law any more than a bill that had only been passed by a lone committee in the U.S. Congress would be a U.S. law.

This caution concerning the non-binding status of this document is echoed by its critics, such as Msgr. Peter J. Elliott, a noted author on the liturgy, who states:

> Published by the U.S. Bishops' Committee on the Liturgy in 1978, this influential document seems dated—insofar as it reflects an era of austere taste. Moreover, together with useful practical advice, it includes unsound opinions regarding the altar (nos. 72–73), the tabernacle (nos. 78–80) and Eucharistic vessels (no. 96) [CMRR 342].

Elsewhere he says:

> A partial reading of authorities and consequent dogmatism is evident in *Environment and Art in Catholic Worship*, 1978, nos. 78, 79. To be fair to the authors, their opinions reflect the era of the 1970s and were presented before *Inaestimabile Donum* and

the new *Code*. But this dated document continues to circulate, endorsed and unmodified [*ibid.*, 325, n. 1].

The Jurist, the canon law journal of the Catholic University of America, published an article in 1996 by the "dean" of liturgical lawyers, Monsignor Frederick R. McManus, titled "Environment and Art in Catholic Worship," which stated:

> [T]he [EACW] statement is not, nor does it purport in any way to be, a law or general decree of the conference of bishops, emanating from the NCCB's legislative power; neither is it a general executory decree of that body. Thus it lacks, and there is no suggestion that it has, juridically binding or obligatory force, for which both two-thirds affirmative vote of the conference's *de jure* membership and the *recognitio* of the Apostolic See are required [*The Jurist* 55:350].

Reasons for Liturgical Abuses

Why do liturgical abuses occur? *Inaestimabile Donum* explained the main cause of the rash of liturgical abuses in this way:

> Most of the difficulties encountered in putting into practice the reform of the liturgy, and especially the reform of the Mass, stem from the fact that neither priests nor faithful have perhaps been sufficiently aware of the theological and spiritual reasons for which the changes have been made, in accordance with the principles laid down by the Council [ID, Conclusion].

It went on to stress the role of priests in correcting the problem:

> Priests must acquire an ever deeper understanding of the authentic way of looking at the Church, of which the celebration of the liturgy, and especially of the Mass, is the living expression. Without an adequate biblical training, priests will not be able to

present to the faithful the meaning of the liturgy as an enactment, in signs, of the history of salvation. Knowledge of the history of the liturgy will likewise contribute to an understanding of the changes which have been introduced, and introduced not for the sake of novelty but as a revival and adaptation of authentic and genuine tradition [*ibid.*].

And in conclusion, *Inaestimabile Donum* stressed the role of liturgical commissions and centers in ending the problem of liturgical abuses:

In the implementation of the liturgical reform, great responsibility falls upon national and diocesan liturgical commissions and liturgical institutes and centers, especially in the work of translating the liturgical books and training the clergy and faithful in the spirit of the reform desired by the Council. The work of these bodies must be at the service of the ecclesiastical authority, which should be able to count upon their faithful collaboration. Such collaboration must be faithful to the Church's norms and directives, and free of arbitrary initiatives and particular ways of acting that could compromise the fruits of the liturgical renewal.

This document will come into the hands of God's ministers in the first decade of the life of the *Missale Romanum* promulgated by Pope Paul VI following the prescriptions of the Second Vatican Council. It seems fitting to recall a remark made by that Pope concerning fidelity to the norms governing celebration: "It is a very serious thing when division is introduced precisely where *congregavit nos in unum Christi amor* ["he calls us together into one love of Christ"], in the Liturgy and the Eucharistic Sacrifice, by the refusing of obedience to the norms laid down in the liturgical sphere" [ID, Conclusion, citing AAS 68 (1976) 374].

2. Ministers at Liturgical Services

In the liturgy, not all people fulfill the same roles. There are a variety of ministers who celebrate or serve at Mass, and all have their own proper functions. In this chapter, we will look at some of the most important ones.

The *General Instruction of the Roman Missal* states:

> All in the assembly gathered for Mass have an individual right and duty to contribute their participation in ways differing according to the diversity of their order and liturgical function. Thus in carrying out this function, all, whether ministers or laypersons, should do all and only those parts that belong to them, so that the very arrangement of the celebration itself makes the Church stand out as being formed in a structure of different orders and ministries [GIRM 58].

It is not necessary, however, that there be a large number of ministers present at Mass:

> If only one minister is present at a Mass with a congregation, he may carry out several different functions [GIRM 72].

But there is a minimum number of ministers which is preferable:

> It is desirable that as a rule an acolyte, a reader, and a cantor assist the priest celebrant; this form of celebration will hereafter be referred to as the "basic" or "typical" form. But the rite described also allows for a greater number of ministers [GIRM 78].

In recent years there has been growing concern over the use of the term "minister" in the Church. In the fullest sense, the term "minister" refers to the ordained—to bishops, priests, and deacons—and that overuse of the term can lead to an erosion of people's understanding of the nature of ordained ministry (ICP, Practical Provisions 1 §2). However, the *Code of Canon Law* and the Church's liturgical documents, in a restricted way, do apply the term "minister" to members of the laity who hold certain offices and fulfill certain functions in the liturgy. The instruction on collaboration states:

> The non-ordained faithful may be generically designated "extraordinary ministers" when deputed by competent authority to discharge, solely by way of supply, those offices mentioned in canon 230 §3 and in canons 943 and 1112. Naturally, the concrete term may be applied to those to whom functions are canonically entrusted, e.g., catechists, acolytes, lectors, etc. [ICP, Practical Provisions 1 §3].

Canon 230 §3 refers to those who, due to lack of ministers such as lectors and acolytes, have been deputed to exercise the ministry of the word regularly, preside over liturgical prayers, confer baptism, and distribute Holy Communion. Canon 943 refers to laity who, in accordance with the requirements of the law, have been deputed to expose and repose the Holy Eucharist regularly. Canon 1112 refers to laity who have been delegated by proper authority to assist at weddings where priests and deacons are lacking.

In all these things, the term "extraordinary minister" may be applied to those who have been deputed to supply these functions *regularly*. The document states:

> Temporary deputation for liturgical purposes . . . does not confer any special or permanent title on the non-ordained faithful [*ibid.*].

It also adds:

It is unlawful for the non-ordained faithful to assume titles such
as "pastor," "chaplain," "coordinator," "moderator" or other
such similar titles which can confuse their role and that of the
Pastor, who is always a Bishop or Priest [*ibid.*].

It is in the senses intended by the Church's legal and liturgical documents that we here use the terms "minister" and
"ministries."

With that said, let us look at some of the more important
ministerial roles at Mass.

Roles of the Ordained

The sacrament of the Holy Eucharist depends in a special way
on the sacrament of holy orders. In order for Mass to be celebrated at all, a bishop or a priest is needed, since only they
can consecrate the elements. Deacons also play an important
role in the liturgy, though their presence is not necessary in
the same way that of a priest or bishop is.

ROLE OF BISHOPS

Because bishops are central to the life of the Church, liturgical celebrations are specially adapted when they are present.
These adaptations are significant enough that there is a special
Church document dealing with liturgical celebrations at which
bishops are present. It is known as the *Ceremonial of Bishops* and
was published by the Congregation for Divine Worship after
Pope John Paul II approved it in 1984. Although we will have
occasion to quote it, we will not focus on the particularly episcopal aspects of it, since bishops do not directly participate in
the majority of Masses that people attend.

Role of Priests

Priests are the principal ministers at Mass, without whom it cannot be celebrated, since those not ordained to the ministerial priesthood are not capable of consecrating the Eucharist. The common or universal priesthood shared by all the Christian faithful is not capable of consecrating the Eucharist.

One of the most important duties of a priest at Mass is the saying of the "presidential prayers:"

> Among the parts assigned to the priest, the Eucharistic prayer is preeminent; it is the high point of the entire celebration. Next are the prayers: the opening prayer or collect, the prayer over the gifts, and the prayer after Communion. The priest, presiding over the assembly in the person of Christ, addresses these prayers to God in the name of the entire holy people and all present. Thus there is a good reason to call them "presidential prayers" [GIRM 10].

It is not appropriate for others to share in these prayers, except as allowed by the liturgical texts that have been approved by the Holy See.

The *Code of Canon Law* states:

Canon 907

> In the celebration of the Eucharist it is not licit for deacons and lay persons to say prayers, in particular the Eucharistic prayer, or to perform actions which are proper to the celebrating priest.

This point was again forcefully reiterated in the recent instruction on collaboration:

> To promote the proper identity (of various roles) in this area, those abuses which are contrary to the provisions of canon 907 are to be eradicated. In Eucharistic celebrations deacons and non-ordained members of the faithful may not pronounce prayers—

e.g. especially the Eucharistic prayer, with its concluding doxology—or any other parts of the liturgy reserved to the celebrant priest. Neither may deacons or non-ordained members of the faithful use gestures or actions which are proper to the same priest celebrant. It is a grave abuse for any member of the non-ordained faithful to "quasi-preside" at the Mass while leaving only that minimal participation to the priest which is necessary to secure validity [ICP, Practical Provisions 6 §1].

The statement that abuses where deacons and lay persons usurp the prayer and gestures of the priests are to be *eradicated*—a word seldom appearing in ecclesiastical documents—shows how serious the Holy See is about this issue.

There are special adaptations made when several priests are saying Mass together—a practice known as concelebration. However, since most Masses that people attend are not concelebrated, we will not be focusing on these adaptations in this book.

ROLE OF DEACONS

In addition to bishops and priests, deacons also share in the sacrament of holy orders, and they have a correspondingly dignified place in the liturgy:

Among ministers, the deacon, whose order has been held in high honor since the early Church, has the first place. At Mass he has his own functions: he proclaims the Gospel, sometimes preaches God's word, leads the general intercessions, assists the priest, gives Communion to the people (in particular, ministering the chalice), and sometimes gives directions regarding the assembly's moving, standing, kneeling, or sitting [GIRM 61].

In general the deacon:

    a. assists the priest and walks at his side;
    b. at the altar, assists with the chalice or the book;

c. if there is no other minister present, carries out other ministerial functions as required [GIRM 127].

The *Ceremonial of Bishops* also stresses the importance of deacons in the Eucharistic celebration:

> Deacons hold the highest place among ministers and from the Church's earliest age the diaconate has been held in great honor. As men of good repute and full of wisdom, they should act in such a way that, with the help of God, all may know them to be true disciples of One who came not to be served but to serve, and who was among his disciples as one who serves.
>
> Strengthened by the gifts of the Holy Spirit, the deacons assist the bishop and his presbyters in the ministry of the word, the altar, and of charity. As ministers of the altar they proclaim the Gospel reading, help at the celebration of the sacrifice, and serve as Eucharistic ministers.
>
> Deacons should therefore look on the bishop as a father and assist him as they would the Lord Jesus Christ himself, who is the eternal High Priest, present in the midst of his people [CB 23–24].

Deacons are permitted to do many things in the liturgy. We cannot treat all these functions here, but they will be discussed at the appropriate points in the chapters on the liturgy of the word and the liturgy of the Eucharist.

Roles Open to Lay Men and Women

Below the level of deacon, there are a number of roles non-ordained people can play in the liturgy. In fact, the non-ordained may perform any function below those reserved to the deacon.

When laity are used to supply special functions in the liturgy and in parish life, a very careful selection and training process must be used:

> Should it become necessary to provide for "supplementary" assistance [by laity as extraordinary ministers of various kinds], the competent authority is bound to select lay faithful of sound doctrine and exemplary moral life. Catholics who do not live worthy lives or who do not enjoy good reputations or whose family situations do not conform to the teaching of the Church may not be admitted to the exercise of such functions. In addition, those chosen should possess that level of formation necessary for the discharge of the responsibilities entrusted to them. . . . Great care must be exercised so that these courses conform absolutely to the teaching of the ecclesiastical Magisterium and they must be imbued with a true spirituality [ICP, Practical Provisions 13].

Lector and acolyte are two historically important offices. They were formerly ranked as "minor orders" and were typically reserved for those in preparation for the reception of sacred orders (cf. DOL 2922).

That changed in 1972, when Pope Paul VI issued a *motu proprio* titled *Ministeria Quaedam* on first tonsure, minor orders, and the subdiaconate (DOL 2922–2938). This document simplified the ministries below that of deacon and, among other things, mandated the following:

> I. First tonsure is no longer conferred; entrance into the clerical state is joined to the diaconate.
>
> II. What up to now were called minor orders are henceforth to be called ministries.
>
> III. Ministries may be assigned to lay Christians; hence they are no longer to be considered as reserved to candidates for the sacrament or orders.

IV. Two ministries, adapted to present-day needs, are to be preserved in the whole Latin church, namely, those of reader [i.e., lector] and acolyte. The functions heretofore assigned to the subdeacon are entrusted to the reader and the acolyte; consequently, the major order of subdiaconate no longer exists in the Latin church. There is, however, no reason why the acolyte cannot be called a subdeacon in some places, at the discretion of the conference of bishops.

V. In accordance with the ancient tradition of the Church, institution to the ministries of reader and acolyte is reserved to men [DOL 2926–2929, 2932].

The continuing nature of the roles of lector and acolyte are also stressed in the *Ceremonial of Bishops:*

The ministries of reader and acolyte are to be preserved in the Latin Church. These ministries may be assigned to the lay Christians and are no longer to be considered as reserved to candidates for the sacrament of orders.

Unless they have already done so, candidates for ordination as deacons and presbyters are to receive these ministries and are to exercise them for a suitable time in order to be better disposed for the future service of the word and of the altar [CB 790].

The requirement that only men serve as formally instituted lectors and acolytes is preserved in the current (1983) *Code of Canon Law:*

CANON 230 §1

Lay men [Latin, *viri*] who possess the age and qualifications determined by decree of the conference of bishops can be installed on a stable basis in the ministries of lector and acolyte in accord with the prescribed liturgical rite. . . .

This does not mean that only formally instituted lectors and acolytes may fulfill these functions:

Laymen, even if they have not received institution as ministers, may perform all the sacred functions below those reserved to deacons . . . [GIRM 70].

Nor does the *Code* mean that women cannot fulfill the functions of lectors and acolytes by temporary deputation. It goes on to state:

CANON 230 §2

Lay persons can fulfill the function of lector during liturgical actions by temporary deputation; likewise all lay persons can fulfill the functions of commentator or cantor or other function, in accord with the norm of law.

In exceptional circumstances, the laity can play still further roles in the liturgy. The Code states:

CANON 230 §3

When the necessity of the Church warrants it and when ministers are lacking, lay persons, even if they are not lectors or acolytes, can also supply for certain of their offices, namely, to exercise the ministry of the word, to preside over liturgical prayers, to confer baptism, and to distribute Holy Communion in accord with the prescriptions of law.

In 1971, the Sacred Congregation for Divine Worship issued the following directive concerning the role of women in the liturgy:

According to the norms established for these matters . . . women are allowed to:

a. proclaim the readings, except the Gospel. . . . The conferences of bishops are to give specific directions on the place best suited for women to read the word of God in the liturgical assembly.

b. announce the intentions in the general intercessions;

c. lead the liturgical assembly in singing and play the organ or other instruments;

d. read the commentary assisting the people toward a better understanding of the rite;

e. attend to other functions, customarily filled by women in other settings, as a service to the congregation, for example, ushering, organizing processions, taking up the collection [*Notitiae* 7 (1971) 10–26, section 7, DOL 525].

The American *Appendix to the General Instruction* has further remarks on the roles of women in the liturgy:

The Conference of Bishops has given permission for women to serve as readers in accord with no. 66 of the *General Instruction* (November, 1969).

In February, 1971, the Bishops' Committee on the Liturgy prepared a commentary on the liturgical ministry of women:

a. With the exception of service at the altar itself, women may be admitted to the exercise of other liturgical ministries. In particular the designation of women to serve in such ministries as reader, cantor, leader of singing, commentator, director of liturgical participation, etc., is left to the judgment of the pastor or the priest who presides over the celebration, in the light of the culture and mentality of the congregation.

b. Worthiness of life and character and other qualifications are required in women who exercise liturgical ministries in the same way as for men who exercise the same ministries.

c. Women who read one or other biblical readings during the liturgy of the word (other than the Gospel, which is reserved to a deacon or priest) should do so from the lectern or ambo where the other readings are proclaimed: the reservation of a single place for all the biblical readings is more significant than the person of the reader, whether ordained or lay, whether woman or man (cf. *General Instruction*, no. 272).

d. Other ministries performed by women, such as leading the singing or otherwise directing the congregation, should be done either within or outside the sanctuary area, depending on the circumstances or convenience [AGI 66].

Today virtually the only role women cannot play in the liturgy, even on the basis of temporary deputation, is found in the symbolic washing of feet performed on Holy Thursday, which reenacts Christ's washing the apostles' feet (John 13:3–20). By Christ's intention, the apostolic college was composed of men. In some places, however, women have been invited to participate in the washing of feet performed on Holy Thursday, but this conflicts with the rubrics for the Mass of Holy Thursday, which state:

> Depending on pastoral circumstances, the washing of feet follows the homily. The men [viri] who have been chosen are led by the ministers to chairs prepared in a suitable place. Then the priest (removing his chasuble if necessary) goes to each man. With the help of the ministers, he pours water over each one's feet and dries them.

The Latin term used above indicates males only. When the term viri appears in Church documents, it indicates that the text is making a requirement for males and not females. If a text intends to include either a male or a female in a requirement, it uses a different Latin term, such as homo, which is not gender-specific.

A 1988 text from the Holy See indicates that the requirement for using men is still in effect:

> The washing of the feet of chosen men [viri] which, according to tradition, is performed on this day, represents the service and charity of Christ, who came "not to be served, but to serve" [Matt. 20:28]. This tradition should be maintained, and its proper significance explained [PS 51].

LECTORS

The office of lector, referred to in some translations as "reader," is an ancient one in the Church. The public reading of Scripture has been part of Christian worship since apostolic times (cf. Col. 4:16, 1 Thess. 5:27, 1 Tim. 4:13). The *Ceremonial of Bishops* remarks:

> The office of reader was historically the first of the lesser ministries to emerge. This office exists in all Churches and has never disappeared. Readers receive institution for an office proper to them: to proclaim the word of God in liturgical assembly. Hence at Mass and in other rites of the liturgy readers proclaim the readings other than the Gospel reading. When there is no cantor of the psalm present, the leader also leads the assembly in the responsorial psalm; when no deacon is present, the reader announces the intentions of the general intercessions.
>
> Whenever necessary, the reader should see to the preparation of any members of the faithful who may be appointed to proclaim the readings from the Sacred Scripture in liturgical celebrations. But in celebrations presided over by the bishop, it is fitting that the readers formally instituted proclaim the readings and, if several readers are present, they should divide the readings accordingly [CB 31].

Though lacking the historical introduction and the adaptation to Masses with bishops, the *General Instruction* describes the basic function of the lector in this way:

> The reader is instituted to proclaim the readings from Scripture, with the exception of the Gospel. He may also announce the intentions for the general intercessions and, in the absence of the psalmist, sing or read the psalm between the readings.
>
> The reader has his own proper function in the Eucharistic celebration and should exercise this even though ministers of a higher rank may be present.

Those who exercise the ministry of reader, even if they have not received institution, must be truly qualified and carefully prepared in order that the faithful will develop a warm and lively love for Scripture from listening to the reading of the sacred texts [GIRM 66].

The *Ceremonial of Bishops* also mentions another function of lectors:

In addition, the reader is entrusted with the special office of instructing children and adults in the faith and of preparing them to receive the sacraments worthily [CB 794].

Lectors are expected to take their duties seriously:

Conscious of the dignity of God's word and the importance of their office, readers should be eager to learn how best to speak and proclaim, in order that those who listen may clearly hear and understand the word of God.

In proclaiming the word of God to others, readers should themselves receive it with docility and meditate on it with devotion so that they may bear witness to the word in their daily lives [CB 32].

Because of their special role at Mass, lectors have a place in the entrance procession at the beginning of the liturgy:

In the procession to the altar, when no deacon is present, the reader may carry the Book of the Gospels. In that case he walks in front of the priest, otherwise he walks with the other ministers.

Upon reaching the altar, the reader makes the proper reverence along with the priest, goes up to the altar, and places the Book of the Gospels on it. Then he takes his place in the sanctuary with the other ministers [GIRM 148–149].

When the time comes to give the Scripture readings, the lector goes to the appointed place:

At the lectern the reader proclaims the readings that precede the Gospel. If there is no cantor of the psalm, he may also sing or recite the responsorial psalm after the first reading [GIRM 150].

The lector may also play a special role during the prayers of the faithful:

After the priest gives the introduction to the general intercession, the reader may announce the intentions when no deacon is present [GIRM 151].

And the lector may play additional roles depending on whether music is used at the Mass:

If there is no entrance song or Communion song and the antiphons in the missal are said by the faithful, the reader recites them at the proper time [GIRM 152].

Cantors

Between the first and second readings at a Sunday Mass is the responsorial psalm. This may be sung or chanted by a cantor:

The cantor of the psalm is to sing the psalm or other biblical song that comes between the readings. To fulfill their function correctly, these cantors should possess singing talent and an aptitude for correct pronunciation and diction [GIRM 67].

The presence of a properly trained cantor is especially desired at Masses at which a bishop presides:

The chants between the readings are very important liturgically and pastorally. It is therefore desirable in celebrations presided over by the bishop, especially in the cathedral church, that there be a psalmist or cantor who has the necessary musical ability and devotion to the liturgy. The cantor of the psalm is responsible for singing, either responsorially or directly, the chants between the readings—the psalm or other biblical canticle, the gradual and *Alleluia*, or other chant—in such a way as to reflect on the meaning of the texts [CB 33].

COMMENTATORS

In many Masses, the celebrating priest will introduce or explain the readings with brief comments. It is permissible, however, for another person—known as a commentator—to do this also:

> The commentator. This minister provides explanations and commentaries with the purpose of introducing the faithful to the celebration and preparing them to understand it better. The commentator's remarks must be meticulously prepared and marked by a simple brevity.
>
> In performing this function the commentator stands in a convenient place visible to the faithful, but it is preferable that this not be at the lectern where the Scriptures are read [GIRM 68a].

Although it is *not* a liturgical abuse for a person other than the priest to introduce the Scripture readings, it *is* a liturgical abuse for a commentator to give a homily (see chapter 5) *or* to use a commentator but omit the homily on days when a homily is mandated, such as Sundays.

ACOLYTES

The role of acolyte is also an ancient one in the Church, and one with specific functions:

> The acolyte is instituted to serve at the altar and to assist the priest and deacon. In particular it is for him to prepare the altar and the vessels and, as [an extraordinary] minister of the Eucharist, to give Communion to the faithful [GIRM 65].

The *Ceremonial of Bishops* also adds two other functions for acolytes—providing necessary instruction for certain other ministers in the liturgy and, in extraordinary cases, exposing the Blessed Sacrament:

> When necessary, acolytes should instruct those who serve as ministers in liturgical rites by carrying the book, the cross, candles, or the censer by performing other similar duties. But in celebrations presided over by the bishop it is fitting that all such ministerial functions be carried out by formally instituted acolytes, and if a number are present, they should divide up the ministry accordingly [CB 28].
>
> In extraordinary circumstances an acolyte may be entrusted with publicly exposing the Blessed Sacrament for adoration by the faithful and afterward replacing it, but not blessing the people with the Blessed Sacrament [CB 808].

An acolyte has a distinct role in the liturgy and should not have this role supplanted by other ministers:

> In the ministry of the altar acolytes have their own proper functions and should exercise these even though ministers of a higher rank may be present [CB 27].

As one of the ministers at Mass, the acolyte has a place in the entrance procession at the beginning of the liturgy:

> In the procession to the altar the acolyte may carry the cross, walking between two servers with lighted candles. When he reaches the altar, he places the cross near it and takes his own place in the sanctuary [GIRM 143].

During the liturgy the acolyte assists the priest and deacon:

> Throughout the celebration it belongs to the acolyte to go to the priest or the deacon, whenever necessary, in order to present the book to them and to assist them in any way required. Thus it is appropriate that, if possible, he have a place from which he

can conveniently carry out his ministry both at the chair and at the altar [GIRM 144].

The acolyte also assists in preparing the altar at the beginning of the liturgy of the Eucharist:

After the general intercessions, when no deacon is present, the acolyte places the corporal, purificator, chalice, and missal at the altar, while the priest remains at the chair. Then, if necessary, the acolyte assists the priest in receiving the gifts of the people and he may bring the bread and wine to the altar and present them to the priest. If incense is used, the acolyte gives the censer to the priest and assists him in incensing the gifts and the altar [GIRM 145].

Acolytes may also serve as extraordinary ministers of Holy Communion:

The acolyte may assist the priest as [an extraordinary] minister in giving Communion to the people. If Communion is given under both kinds, the acolyte ministers the chalice to the communicants, or he holds the chalice when Communion is being given by intinction [GIRM 146].

The acolyte may also play a role in purifying the vessels after Communion (see the section on the purification of the vessels in chapter 8 for more information):

After Communion, the acolyte helps the priest or deacon to purify and arrange the vessels. If no deacon is present, the acolyte takes the vessels to the side table where he purifies and arranges them [GIRM 147].

Extraordinary Ministers of Holy Communion

The ordinary ministers of Communion are priests and deacons. Instituted acolytes are *de iure* (by law) extraordinary ministers of the Eucharist. Other lay persons are authorized to act as extraordinary ministers of Holy Communion by the Holy See's 1973 instruction *Immensae Caritatis:*

I. Local Ordinaries [normally the bishop] possess the faculty enabling them to permit fit persons, each chosen by name as [an extraordinary[1]] minister, in a given instance or for a set period or even permanently, to give Communion to themselves and others of the faithful and to carry it to the sick residing at home:

a. whenever no priest, deacon, or acolyte is available;

b. whenever the same ministers are impeded from administering Communion because of another pastoral ministry, ill-health, or old age;

c. whenever the number of faithful wishing to receive Communion is so great that the celebration of Mass or the giving of Communion outside Mass would take too long.

II. The same local Ordinaries possess the faculty of granting individual priests in the course of their ministry the power to

---

[1] The DOL uses a translation prepared by the International Committee on English in the Liturgy (ICEL) which is misleading when translating the phrase "extraordinary ministers of Holy Communion" and its variants. In an attempt to deprive the position of its extraordinary character, the responsible party or parties at ICEL systematically mistranslated the term "extraordinary" (*extraordinarius*) as "special" (which, in Latin, would be *peculiaris*). Here and in the other citations from DOL, we have restored the correct term in square brackets. The problem also appears in some editions of the Sacramentary, and we have followed the same procedure restoring the correct term.

appoint, for a given occasion, a fit person to distribute Communion in cases of genuine necessity.

. . . Because these faculties have been granted exclusively in favor of the spiritual good of the faithful and for cases of genuine need, let priests remember that such faculties do not release them from the obligation of giving the Eucharist to the faithful who lawfully request it and especially of bringing and administering it to the sick.

The faithful who are [extraordinary] ministers of Communion must be persons whose good qualities of Christian life, faith, and morals recommend them. Let them strive to be worthy of this great office, foster their own devotion to the Eucharist, and show an example to the rest of the faithful by their own devotion and reverence toward the most august sacrament of the altar. No one is to be chosen whose appointment the faithful might find disquieting [IC 1, DOL 2075–2076, 2081].

Some have expressed concern about the overuse of extraordinary ministers. This was clarified in *Inaestimabile Donum*:

The faithful, whether religious or lay, who are authorized as extraordinary ministers of the Eucharist can distribute Communion only when there is no priest, deacon, or acolyte, when the priest is impeded by illness or advanced age, or when the number of the faithful going to Communion is so large as to make the celebration of Mass excessively long. Accordingly, a reprehensible attitude is shown by those priests who, though present at the celebration, refrain from distributing Communion and leave this task to the laity [ID 10].

Special attention has also been paid to the overuse of extraordinary ministers in the United States. In 1987, after receiving numerous complaints about too frequent use of extraordinary ministers, the Congregation of Sacraments sent a *dubium* to the Pontifical Commission for the Authentic Interpretation of the *Code of Canon Law* asking the following:

Whether the extraordinary minister of Holy Communion, appointed according to c. 910, §2, and 230, §3, may exercise his supplementary task when there are present in the church, even if they are not participating in the celebration of the Eucharist, unimpeded ordinary ministers [*Roman Replies and CLSA Advisory Opinions* 1988:4].

In a plenary session on February 20, 1987, the Pontifical Commission replied: "In the Negative" (*ibid.*, 5). Cardinal Augustin Mayer, Prefect of the Congregation of Sacraments, then communicated this decision in a circular letter to the various papal representatives. In response, the Apostolic Pro-Nuncio to the United States sent a letter to the president of the U.S. National Conference of Catholic Bishops, in which he explained:

> Such abuses have led to situations where the *extraordinary* character of this ministry has been lost. At times, it also appears as though the designation of extraordinary ministers becomes a kind of reward to repay those who have worked for the Church [*ibid.*].

Cardinal Mayer notes that the abuses he speaks of happen if:
—the extraordinary ministers of the Eucharist *ordinarily* distribute Holy Communion together with the celebrant, both when the number of communicants would not require their assistance, and when there are other concelebrants or other ordinary ministers available, though not celebrating;
—the extraordinary ministers distribute Holy Communion to themselves and to the faithful while the celebrant and concelebrants, if there are any, remain inactive. . . .

The reply of the Pontifical Commission clearly indicates that, when ordinary ministers (bishop, priest, deacon) are present at the Eucharist, whether they are celebrating or not, and are in sufficient number and not prevented from doing so by other ministries, the extraordinary ministers of the Eucharist are not allowed to distribute Communion either to themselves or to the faithful [*ibid.*, 6–7].

The recent instruction on collaboration also addressed the overuse of extraordinary ministers of Holy Communion:

> A non-ordained member of the faithful, in cases of true necessity, may be deputed by the diocesan bishop, using the appropriate form of blessing for these situations, to act as an extraordinary minister to distribute Holy Communion outside of liturgical celebrations *ad actum vel ad tempus* ["for a particular occasion or for a time"] or for a more stable period. In exceptional cases or in unforeseen circumstances, the priest presiding at the liturgy may authorize such *ad actum* ["for a particular occasion"; ICP, Practical Provisions 8 §1].

The role of extraordinary ministers inside Mass is also addressed:

> Extraordinary ministers may distribute Holy Communion at Eucharistic celebrations only when there are no ordained ministers present or when those ordained ministers present at a liturgical celebration are truly unable to distribute Holy Communion. They may also exercise this function at Eucharistic celebrations where there are particularly large numbers of the faithful and which would be excessively prolonged because of an insufficient number of ordained ministers to distribute Holy Communion. . . .

> To avoid creating confusion, certain practices are to be avoided and eliminated where such have emerged in particular Churches [including] . . . the habitual use of extraordinary ministers of Holy Communion at Mass thus arbitrarily extending the concept of "a great number of the faithful" [*ibid.*, 8 §2].

The strong phrasing—saying that the habitual use of extraordinary ministers is to be *eliminated*—again shows the seriousness of the Holy See about this issue.

To help promote the correct use of extraordinary ministers, the document suggests that the local bishop draft norms—in accordance with the universal law of the Church—to help explain how extraordinary ministers of Holy Communion are to be used and how they are to perform their role:

> This function is *supplementary and extraordinary* and must be exercised in accordance with the norm of law. It is thus useful for the diocesan bishop to issue particular norms concerning extraordinary ministers of Holy Communion which, in complete harmony with the universal law of the Church, should regulate the exercise of this function in his diocese. Such norms should provide, amongst other things, for matters such as the instruction in Eucharistic doctrine of those chosen to be extraordinary ministers of Holy Communion, the meaning of the service they provide, the rubrics to be observed, the reverence to be shown for such an august Sacrament and instruction concerning the discipline on admission to Holy Communion [*ibid.*].

Lay women were permitted to be extraordinary ministers of Holy Communion in 1969. The Holy See ruled:

> A lay Christian who is to be chosen as [an extraordinary] minister of Communion should be outstanding in Christian life, in faith, and in morals, and one whose mature age warrants the choice and who is properly trained to carry out so exalted a function. A woman of outstanding piety may be chosen in cases of necessity, that is, whenever another fit person cannot be found [FC 5, DOL 2048].

This role has been expanded to be as open for women as for men. The Holy See's 1973 instruction *Immensae Caritatis* made no differentiation between men and women as extraordinary ministers of Holy Communion:

> [Extraordinary ministers of Holy Communion] will be designated according to the order of this listing (which may be changed at the prudent discretion of the local ordinary): reader, major seminarian, man religious, woman religious, catechist, one of the faithful—a man or a woman [IC 1:IV, DOL 2078].

All the same rules regarding male extraordinary ministers of Holy Communion also apply to women (e.g., the rules regarding the occasions on which extraordinary ministers may be used and what they may wear).

ALTAR SERVERS

In recent years, significant controversy has surrounded the question of whether there can be female altar servers, especially altar girls. The Church created the position of altar server centuries ago to allow boys to serve in the place of acolytes at the altar. However, altar servers do not perform *all* functions of acolytes—such as distributing Communion, which they do not do unless they are also extraordinary ministers of Holy Communion.

In 1994, when the Holy See allowed national conferences of bishops to decide whether to permit female altar servers in their jurisdiction. In an audience granted on July 11, 1992, Pope John Paul II approved a response the Pontifical Council for the Interpretation of Legal Texts had given to an inquiry concerning the meaning of canon 230 §2 in the *Code of Canon Law*, which states:

> Lay persons can fulfill the function of lector during liturgical actions by temporary deputation; likewise all lay persons can fulfill the functions of commentator or cantor or other functions, in accord with the norm of law.

The Council was asked whether this canon is to be interpreted to mean that both men and women may perform these functions and if the functions include serving at the altar for both men and women.

The Council said yes on both counts, and the decision was published in the journal of the Congregation for Divine Worship and the Discipline of the Sacraments, *Notitiae* (June–July 1994, 346–347). Along with this was published a clarification by Cardinal Javierre Ortas (*ibid.*, 347–348). The same two pieces were also published in the June 6, 1994, issue of *Acta Apostolicae Sedis* (86:6:541–542).

Some have tried to argue against the legality of female altar servers by claiming that the documents were not properly signed, were not properly approved by the Pope, or were not published in the proper journals. None of these things are true. The Pope did approve the response given on canon 230 §2. The documents were signed both by the prefects and the secretaries of the relevant bodies. And they were published in *Notitiae,* the record of the congregation that has oversight of the sacraments, and *Acta Apostolicae Sedis,* the official record in which the Holy See publishes the laws, decrees, and acts of congregations and tribunals in the Roman Curia. There is no doubt concerning the *legality* of female altar servers, however one may feel about the appropriateness or prudence of their use.

The two pieces were summarized and communicated to the presidents of the bishops' conferences by Cardinal Ortas:

Rome, 15 March 1994

Excellence,

It is my duty to communicate to the presidents of the episcopal conferences that an authentic interpretation of canon 230 §2 of the *Code of Canon Law* will soon be published in *Acta Apostolicae Sedis.*

As you know, canon 230 §2 lays down that:

"*Laici ex temporanea deputatione in actionibus liturgicis munus lectoris implere possunt; item omnes laici muneribus commentatoris, cantoris aliisve ad normam iuris fungi possunt.*"

The Pontifical Council for the interpretation of Legislative Texts was recently asked if the liturgical functions which, according to the above canon, can be entrusted to the lay faithful, may be carried out equally by men and women, and if serving at the altar may be included among those functions, on a par with the others indicated by the canon.

At its meeting of 30 June 1992, the members of the Pontifical Council for the Interpretation of Legislative Texts examined the following *dubium* which had been proposed to them:

> "*Utrum inter munera liturgica quibus laici, sive viri sive mulieres, iuxta CIC can. 230 §2, fungi possunt, adnumerari etiam possit servitium ad altare.*"

The following response was given: "*Affirmative et iuxta instructiones a Sede Apostolica dandas.*"

Subsequently, at an audience granted on 11 July 1992 to the Most Reverend Vincenzo Fagiolo, Archbishop Emeritus of Chieti-Vasto and President of the Pontifical Council for the Interpretation of Legislative Texts, Pope John Paul II confirmed the decision and ordered its promulgation. This will be done in the near future.

In communicating the above information to your episcopal conference, I feel obliged to clarify certain aspects of canon 230 §2 and of its authentic interpretation:

1) Canon 230 §2 has a permissive and not a preceptive character: "*Laici . . . possunt.*" Hence the permission given in this regard by some bishops can in no way be considered as binding on other bishops. In fact, it is the competence of each bishop, in his diocese, after hearing the opinion of the episcopal conference, to make a prudential judgment on what to do, with a view to the ordered development of liturgical life in his own diocese.

2) The Holy See respects the decision adopted by certain bishops for specific local reasons on the basis of the provisions of canon 230 §2. At the same time, however, the Holy See wishes to recall that it will always be very appropriate to fol-

low the noble tradition of having boys serve at the altar. As is well known, this has led to a reassuring development of priestly vocations. Thus the obligation to support such groups of altar boys will always continue.

3) If in some diocese, on the basis of canon 230 §2, the bishop permits that, for particular reasons, women may also serve at the altar, this decision must be clearly explained to the faithful, in the light of the above-mentioned norm. It shall also be made clear that the norm is already being widely applied, by the fact that women frequently serve as lectors in the liturgy and can also be called upon to distribute Holy Communion as extraordinary ministers of the Eucharist and to carry out other functions, according to the provisions of the same canon 230 §3.

4) It must also be clearly understood that the liturgical services mentioned above are carried out by lay people "*ex temporanea deputatione,*" according to the judgment of the bishop, without lay people, be they men or women, having any right to exercise them.

In communicating the above, the Congregation for Divine Worship and the Discipline of the Sacraments has sought to carry out the mandate received from the Supreme Pontiff to provide directives to illustrate what is laid down in canon 230 §2 of the *Code of Canon Law* and its authentic interpretation, which will shortly be published.

In this way the bishops will be better able to carry out their mission to be moderators and promoters of liturgical life in their own dioceses, within the framework of the norms in force of the Universal Church.

In deep communion with all the members of your Episcopal Conference. I remain,

Yours sincerely in Christ,

Cardinal Antonio Maria Javierre Ortas
Prefect
Sacred Congregation for Divine Worship
and the Discipline of the Sacraments

The Role of Children

Particular norms governing Masses in which a large number of children participates are set down in a 1973 document put out by the Holy See's then Congregation for Divine Worship. The document, titled *Directory for Masses with Children,* authorizes special adaptations for Masses involving children.

These adaptations vary depending on whether the number of adults at Mass is great or whether only a few adults are participating. Concerning Masses where adults predominate, the *Directory* states:

> In many places parish Masses are celebrated, especially on Sundays and holy days, at which a good many children take part along with the large number of adults. On such occasions the witness of adult believers can have a great effect upon the children. Adults can in turn benefit spiritually from experiencing the part that the children have within the Christian community. The Christian spirit of the family is greatly fostered when children take part in these Masses together with their parents and other family members [DMC 16].

While it is desirable that children take part in the entire Mass along with their parents, other arrangements are possible. The *Directory* goes on to state:

> Infants who as yet are unable or unwilling to take part in the Mass may be brought in at the end of Mass to be blessed together with the rest of the community. This may be done, for example, if parish helpers have been taking care of them in a separate area [*ibid.*].

It is also important to make the children feel at home in Masses at which adults predominate:

> [I]n Masses of this kind it is necessary to take great care that the children present do not feel neglected because of their in-

ability to participate or to understand what happens and what
is proclaimed in the celebration. Some account should be taken
of their presence: for example, by speaking to them directly in
the introductory comments (as at the beginning and the end of
Mass) and at some point in the homily [DMC 17].

It is also an authorized practice for parishes to have a separate celebration of the liturgy of the word for children:

> Sometimes, moreover, if the place itself and the nature of the
> community permit, it will be appropriate to celebrate the liturgy
> of the word, including a homily, with the children in a separate,
> but not too distant room. Then, before the Eucharistic liturgy
> begins, the children are led to the place where the adults have
> meanwhile celebrated their own liturgy of the word [DMC 17].

It is also permissible for children to perform certain roles at
Masses at which adults participate:

> It may also be very helpful to give some tasks to the children.
> They may, for example, bring forward the gifts or perform one
> or other of the songs of the Mass [DMC 18].

There are even cases when the degree of adaptation ap-
proaches that given to Masses at which children predominate:

> If the number of children is large, it may at times be suitable to
> plan the Mass so that it corresponds more closely to the needs
> of the children. In this case the homily should be directed to
> them but in such a way that the adults may also benefit from it.
> Where the bishop permits, in addition to the adaptations already
> provided in the Order of Mass, one or other of the particular
> adaptations described later in the Directory may be employed in
> a Mass celebrated with adults in which children also participate
> [DMC 19].

These circumstances, however, are uncommon. It is more
common for there to be a Mass with a large number of children

and only a few adults present during the week, for example, at a Catholic school. For such cases, the *Directory for Masses with Children* has a different set of adaptations. The document recommends the use of the special adaptations for these Masses, but it also cautions against too many modifications:

> In addition to the Masses in which children take part with their parents and other family members (which are not always possible everywhere), Masses with children in which only a few adults take part are recommended, especially during the week. . . .
>
> It is always necessary to keep in mind that these Eucharistic celebrations must lead children toward the celebration of Mass with adults, especially the Masses at which the Christian community must come together on Sundays. Thus, apart from adaptations that are necessary because of the children's age, the result should not be entirely special rites, markedly different from the Order of Mass celebrated with a congregation. The purpose of the various elements should always correspond with what is said in the *General Instruction of the Roman Missal* on individual points, even if at times for pastoral reasons an absolute *identity* cannot be insisted upon [DMC 20–21].

Because these Masses are not ones which adults commonly experience, we will not go into detail concerning these adaptations, though they include more roles for the children, such as allowing them to give the Scripture readings (except, of course, for the Gospel, which is still reserved to a priest or deacon).

For those who wish to read more concerning Masses with children in which only a few adults participate, a copy of the *Directory for Masses with Children* should be available at any local parish, and especially parishes that operate Catholic schools.

3. Preparation for Mass

Before Mass begins, it is necessary to prepare the altar and the various articles that will be used during Mass. Maintaining the church's cleanliness ensures that it is a beautiful and dignified place for celebrating Mass. The *Ceremonial of Bishops* states:

> The first of all the elements belonging to the beauty of the place where the liturgy is celebrated is the spotless cleanliness of the floor and walls and of all the images and articles that will be used during a service. In all the liturgical appurtenances both ostentation and shabbiness are to be avoided; instead the norms of noble simplicity, refinement, gracefulness, and artistic excellence are to be respected. The culture of the people and the local tradition should guide the choice of objects and their arrangement, "on condition that they serve the places of worship and sacred rites with the reverence and honor due them."
>
> The adornment and décor of a church should always be such as to make the church a visible sign of love and reverence toward God of the real meaning of the feasts celebrated there and to inspire in them a sense of joy and devotion [CB 38].

For additional information concerning liturgical furnishings, see chapter 10.

Preparation of General Liturgical Furnishings

When preparations are being made for a normal celebration of Mass, the following is directed:

The altar is to be covered with at least one cloth. On or near the altar there are to be candlesticks with lighted candles, at least two but even four, six, or, if the bishop of the diocese celebrates, seven. There is also to be a cross on or near the altar. The candles and cross may be carried in the entrance procession. The Book of the Gospels, if distinct from the book of the other readers, may be placed on the altar, unless it is carried in the entrance procession.

The following should also be prepared:

a. next to the priest's chair: the missal and, as may be useful, a book with the chants;

b. at the lectern: the Lectionary;

c. on a side table: the chalice, corporal, purificator, and, if useful, a pall; a paten and ciboria, if needed, with the bread for the Communion of the ministers and the people, together with cruets containing wine and water, unless all of these are brought in by the faithful at the presentation of the gifts; Communion plate for the Communion of the faithful; the requisites for the washing of hands. The chalice should be covered with a veil, which may always be white [GIRM 79–80].

There are special preparations to be made at certain times of the liturgical year—for example, during penitential seasons:

During Lent the Altar is not to be decorated with flowers and the use of musical instruments is allowed only to support singing. The fourth Sunday of Lent, called Laetare Sunday, solemnities and feasts are exceptions to this rule. On Laetare Sunday rose vestments may be used [CB 252].

It is a custom in some countries (though not in the U.S.; see p. 246) to veil the crosses in a church on the Saturday before the fifth Sunday of Lent:

The practice of covering the crosses and images in the church may be observed if the episcopal conference should so decide. The crosses are to be covered until the end of the celebration of the Lord's passion on Good Friday. Images are to remain covered until the beginning of the Easter Vigil [PS 26].

Following the Mass of the Lord's Supper on Holy Thursday, the altar is stripped:

After Mass the altar should be stripped. It is fitting that any crosses in the church be covered with a red or purple veil, unless they have already been veiled on the Saturday before the fifth Sunday of Lent. Lamps should not be lit before the images of saints [PS 57].

The altar is still bare when the Good Friday liturgy is begun, and following the liturgy it is again stripped:

After the celebration, the altar is stripped; the cross remains, however, with four candles. An appropriate place (for example, the chapel of repose used for reservation of the Eucharist on Maundy Thursday) can be prepared within the church, and there the Lord's cross is placed so that the faithful may venerate and kiss it, and spend some time in meditation [PS 71].

The altar is left bare on Holy Saturday. The rubrics for Holy Saturday in the Sacramentary state:

On Holy Saturday the Church waits at the Lord's tomb, meditating on his suffering and death. The altar is left bare, and the sacrifice of the Mass is not celebrated. Only after the solemn vigil during the night, held in anticipation of the resurrection, does the Easter celebration begin, with a spirit of joy that overflows into the following period of fifty days.

On this day Holy Communion may be given only as viaticum.

Though not stripped on All Souls Day, the altar's adornments are similarly diminished:

On All Souls there are no flowers on the altar, and the use of the organ and other instruments is permitted only to sustain the singing [CB 397].

For further information on the proper preparations for Mass on specific days of the liturgical year, see the rubrics of the Sacramentary.

Preparation of Incense

If incense is to be used at Mass, it also will need to be prepared. The purpose of using incense in Mass is explained in the *Ceremonial of Bishops:*

> The rite of incensation or thurification is a sign of reverence and of prayer, as is clear from Psalm 141(140):2 and Revelation 8:3 [CB 84].

Though not as common as it was, incense is still permitted at any Mass. The *General Instruction* states:

> The use of incense is optional in any form of Mass:
> a. during the entrance procession;
> b. at the beginning of Mass, to incense the altar;
> c. at the procession and proclamation of the Gospel;
> d. at the preparation of the gifts, to incense them, as well as the altar, priest, and people;
> e. at the showing of the Eucharistic bread and chalice after the consecration [GIRM 235].

The use of incense is recommended on a number of occasions:

> In addition, incense should be used as a rule during the procession for the feast of the Presentation of the Lord, Passion Sunday (Palm Sunday), the Mass of the Lord's Supper, the Easter Vigil, the solemnity of the Body and Blood of Christ (Corpus Christi), and the solemn translation of relics, and in general, in any procession of some solemnity [CB 88].

Concerning the type of incense that is to be used, the *Ceremonial of Bishops* states:

The substance placed in the censer should be pure sweet—scented incense alone or at least in larger portion than any additive mixed with the incense [CB 85].

And regarding the use of incense, the *General Instruction* states:

The priest puts the incense in the censer and blesses it with the sign of the cross, saying nothing.
    This is the way to incense the altar:
    a. If the altar is freestanding, the priest incenses it as he walks around it.
    b. If the altar is not freestanding, he incenses it while walking first to the right side, then to the left.
    If there is a cross on or beside the altar, he incenses it before he incenses the altar. If the cross is behind the altar, the priest incenses it when he passes in front of it [GIRM 236].
    If a deacon is present, he has a role helping the priest with the incense, most notably at the reading of the Gospel:
    If incense is used, the deacon assists the priest when he puts incense in the censer during the singing of the *Alleluia* or other chant. Then he bows before the priest and asks for the blessing, saying in a low voice: *Father give me your blessing.* The priest then blesses him: *The Lord be in your heart.* The deacon answers: *Amen.* If the Book of the Gospels is on the altar, he takes it and goes to the lectern; the servers, if there are any, precede, carrying candles and the censer when used. At the lectern the deacon greets the people, incenses the book, and proclaims the Gospel. After the reading, he kisses the book, saying inaudibly: *May the words of the Gospel wipe away our sins*, and returns to the priest. If there is no homily or profession of faith, he may remain at the lectern for the general intercessions, but the servers leave [GIRM 131].

The deacon also plays a role in the use of incense at other times, as do other ministers, especially if a deacon is not present. For more information, consult the rubrics in the Sacramentary.

Preparation of the Hosts to Be Consecrated

The elements that will be consecrated during Mass should be prepared beforehand. In order to have a licit and valid celebration of the Eucharist, very specific kinds of elements must be used. The *Code of Canon Law* states:

CANON 924 §1

The Most Sacred Eucharistic Sacrifice must be celebrated with bread and wine, with which a small quantity of water is to be mixed.

Any celebration of the Eucharist that does not use bread and wine of the type described in the *Code of Canon Law* (see below) is *illicit*, meaning it is not permitted. If the deviation from the requisite type of bread and wine is substantial enough, the celebration of the sacrament will be *invalid*, meaning that the elements do not become the Body and Blood of Christ when the priest says the words of consecration.

INGREDIENTS OF THE HOST

Concerning the kind of bread that is to be used, the *Code of Canon Law* states:

CANON 924 §2

The bread must be made of wheat alone and recently made so that there is no danger of corruption.

In most of the Eastern Rite Catholic churches, leavened bread is mandated. This is a legitimate difference between the Eastern and Western parts of the Catholic Church. However, leavened bread is not permitted in Latin Rite Catholic churches, which are considerably more common in Europe and the Americas. In Latin Rite churches,

> [t]he bread must be made only from wheat and must have been baked recently; according to the long-standing tradition of the Latin Church, it must be unleavened [GIRM 282].

This is also specifically mandated by the *Code of Canon Law:*

CANON 926

> In accord with the ancient tradition of the Latin Church, the priest is to use unleavened bread in the celebration of the Eucharist whenever he offers it.

The nature of the bread to be consecrated is further elaborated in *Inaestimabile Donum:*

> The bread for the celebration of the Eucharist, in accordance with the tradition of the whole Church, must be made solely of wheat, and, in accordance with the tradition proper to the Latin Church, it must be unleavened. By reason of the sign, the matter of the Eucharistic celebration "should appear as actual food." This is to be understood as linked to the consistency of the bread, and not to its form, which remains the traditional one [i.e., the form of a wafer]. No other ingredients are to be added to the wheaten flour and water. The preparation of the bread requires attentive care to ensure that the product does not detract from the dignity due to the Eucharistic bread, can be broken in a dignified way, does not give rise to excessive fragments, and does not offend the sensibilities of the faithful when they eat it [ID 8].

Fr. Nicholas Halligan, a leading sacramental theologian, describes what may be considered invalid matter:

The bread must be made from wheat, mixed with natural water, baked by the application of fire heat (including electric cooking) and substantially uncorrupted. The variety of the wheat or the region of its origin does not affect its validity, but bread made from any other grain is invalid matter. Bread made with milk, wine, oil, etc., either entirely or in a notable part, is invalid material. Any natural water suffices for validity, e.g., even mineral water or sea water. The addition of a condiment, such as salt or sugar, is unlawful but valid, unless added in a notable quantity. Unbaked dough or dough fried in butter or cooked in water is invalid matter; likewise bread which is corrupted substantially, but not if it has merely begun to corrupt. Therefore, the valid material of this sacrament must be in the common estimation of reasonable men bread made from wheat and not mixed notably with something else so that it is no longer wheat. Those who make altar breads must be satisfied that they have purchased genuine and pure wheat flour. . . . It is gravely unlawful to consecrate with doubtful matter [*The Sacraments and Their Celebration*, 65–66].

Low-Gluten Hosts

In recent years, the question has arisen as to what provision can be made for sufferers of celiac sprue disease, which causes the gluten found in regular wheat to irritate the intestinal lining of the sufferers. One traditional solution has been to offer celiac sufferers Communion under the species of wine only. However, provision has also been made for the use of low-gluten altar breads. The most recent regulations were approved by the Congregation for the Doctrine of the Faith on June 22, 1994, and distributed in a letter by Cardinal Ratzinger:

I. Concerning permission to use low-gluten altar breads:

A. This may be granted by ordinaries to priests and laypersons affected by celiac disease, after presentation of a medical certificate.

B. Conditions for the validity of the matter:

1) Special hosts *quibus glutinum ablatum est* [from which gluten has been removed] are invalid matter for the celebration of the Eucharist.

2) Low-gluten hosts are valid matter, provided that they contain the amount of gluten sufficient to obtain the confection of bread, that there is no addition of foreign materials, and that the procedure for making such hosts is not such as to alter the nature of the substance of the bread. . . .

III. Common norms

A. The ordinary must ascertain that the matter used conforms to the above requirements.

B. Permissions are to be given only for as long as the situation continues which motivated the request.

C. Scandal is to be avoided [*Origins* (1996) 25:47:192].

Shape of the Host

Regarding the shape of the bread to be consecrated, the *General Instruction* states:

The nature of the sign demands that the material for the Eucharistic celebration truly have the appearance of food. Accordingly, even though unleavened and baked in the traditional shape, the Eucharistic bread should be made in such a way that in a Mass with a congregation the priest is able actually to break the host into parts and distribute them to at least some of the faithful. (When, however, the number of communicants is large or other pastoral needs require it, small hosts are in no way ruled out.) The action of the breaking of the bread, the simple term for the Eucharist in apostolic times, will more clearly bring out the force and meaning of the sign of the unity of all in the one bread and of their charity, since one bread is being distributed among the members of one family [GIRM 283].

Because of confusion over this passage, which led to some priests abandoning the use of standard, wafer-like hosts for the Eucharist (or at least for the priest's host), the Holy See issued a clarification of this passage:

Query: In the GIRM no. 283, what does Eucharistic bread mean?

Reply: The term means the same thing as the *host* hitherto in use, except that the bread is larger in size. The term *Eucharistic bread* in line 2 is explained by the words of line 4: "The priest is able actually *to break the host into parts.*" Thus line 2 is about this Eucharistic element as to its *kind* and line 4 as to its *shape*. Therefore it was incorrect to interpret *Eucharistic bread* in line 2 as a reference to its shape as though the term implies that bread in the shape designed for its everyday use may be substituted for the host in its traditional shape [i.e., a wafer]. The GIRM in no way intended to change the shape of the large and small hosts, but only to provide an option regarding size, thickness, and color in order that the host may really have the appearance of bread that is shared by many people [*Notitiae* 6 (1970) 37, no. 24].

That the hosts normally have the traditional, wafer shape was also stressed in *Inaestimabile Donum* (see quotation above).

Preparation of Wine to Be Consecrated

GENERAL TYPE OF WINE

Just as the kind of hosts that are to be used at Mass are carefully stipulated, so is the kind of wine. The *Code of Canon Law* states:

CANON 924 §3

> The wine must be natural wine of the grape and not corrupt.

This is further elaborated in *Inaestimabile Donum*:

> Faithful to Christ's example, the Church has constantly used bread and wine mixed with water to celebrate the Lord's Supper. . . . The wine for the Eucharistic celebration must be of "the fruit of the vine" (Luke 22:18) and be natural and genuine, that is to say, not mixed with other substances [ID 8].

In discussing what may be considered invalid matter for the wine, Fr. Halligan states:

> To be valid material, wine must be made from ripe grapes of the vine and not substantially corrupted; it cannot come from any other fruits or from unripe grapes or from the stems and skins of the grapes after all the juice has been pressed out. In regions where fresh grapes cannot be obtained, it is lawful to use raisin wine, i.e., wine made by adding water to raisins. Wine from which all alcohol has been removed or which on the other hand has more than twenty percent alcohol or to which foreign ingredients (e.g., water) have been added in equal or greater quantities is invalid material. Wine is likewise invalid which has turned to acid or which is not natural but was manufactured by some chemical process, i.e., by mixing the constituents found in wine so that the product resembles wine. Wine must also be

in a potable [i.e., drinkable] state, and thus if it is congealed (although most probably valid), it must be melted. The color, strength, or origin of wine does not affect its validity.

It is gravely unlawful to use doubtful material, and thus it is unlawful to consecrate wine which is just beginning to turn sour or to corrupt. Wine must be naturally fermented and the use of "must" (unfermented grape juice) is gravely unlawful. To be lawful, wine must be pure, free from the lees, diseases, and foreign ingredients. Lawful wine may not contain more than eighteen percent alcohol (obtained from the grape); wines which would not ordinarily ferment beyond twelve percent alcohol cannot be fortified beyond this limit. The Holy See has been insistent that the sacramental or Mass wine come from sources beyond suspicion, since there are many ways in which wine can be vitiated or adulterated, many methods which are actually used in this country to preserve, age, ameliorate wines. Wines should be purchased regularly only from reputable vendors of Mass wine or only when otherwise guaranteed to be pure and unadulterated [op. cit., 66–67].

Non-Alcoholic Wine

In recent years, attention has been paid to the possible sacramental use of unfermented grape juice, called "must" or "mustum," by priests who suffer from alcoholism. The current regulations, expressed in the same letter from Cardinal Ratzinger mentioned above, are as follows:

II. Concerning permission to use "mustum:"

A. The preferred solution continues to be Communion *per intinctionem* ["by intinction"], or in concelebration under the species of bread alone.

B. Nevertheless, the permission to use *mustum* can be granted by ordinaries to priests affected by alcoholism or other conditions which prevent the ingestion of even the smallest quantity of alcohol, after presentation of a medical certificate.

C. By *mustum* is understood fresh juice from grapes or juice preserved by suspending its fermentation (by means of freezing or other methods which do not alter its nature).

D. In general, those who have received permission to use *mustum* are prohibited from presiding at concelebrated Masses. There may be some exceptions, however: in the case of a bishop or superior general; or, with prior approval of the ordinary, at the concelebration of the anniversary of priestly ordination or other similar occasions. In these cases the one who presides is to communicate under both the species of bread and that of *mustum*, while for the other celebrants a chalice shall be provided in which normal wine is to be consecrated.

E. In the very rare instances of laypersons requesting this permission, recourse must be made to the Holy See [*op. cit.*].

In addition to the common norms given above for the use of low-gluten altar breads, the letter also specified:

D. Given the centrality of the celebration of the Eucharist in the life of the priest, candidates for the priesthood who are affected by celiac disease or suffer from alcoholism or similar conditions may not be admitted to holy orders [*ibid.*].

4. Introductory Rites

Entrance Procession

The *General Instruction* specifies that for the basic form of the celebration of Mass, the introductory rites begin in this way:

> Once the congregation has gathered, the priest and the ministers, clad in their vestments, go to the altar in this order:
>
> a. a server with a lighted censer, if incense is used;
>
> b. the servers, who, according to the occasion, carry lighted candles, and between them the crossbearer, if the cross is to be carried;
>
> c. acolytes and other ministers;
>
> e. a reader, who may carry the Book of the Gospels;
>
> f. the priest who is to celebrate the Mass.
>
> If incense is used, the priest puts some in the censer before the procession begins.
>
> During the procession to the altar the entrance song is sung . . . [GIRM 82–83].

If a deacon is present, he also takes part in the entrance procession:

> Vested and carrying the Book of the Gospels, the deacon precedes the priest on the way to the altar or else walks at the priest's side [GIRM 128].

The *General Instruction* also clarifies the purpose of the entrance song and how it is to be sung:

> After the people have assembled, the entrance song begins as the priest and the ministers come in. The purpose of this song

is to open the celebration, intensify the unity of the gathered people, lead their thoughts to the mystery of the season or feast, and accompany the procession of priest and ministers.

The entrance song is sung alternately either by the choir and the congregation or by the cantor and the congregation; or it is sung entirely by the congregation or by the choir alone. The antiphon and psalm of the *Graduale Romanum* or the Simple Gradual may be used, or another song that is suited to this part of the Mass, the day, or the seasons and that has a text approved by the conference of bishops.

If there is no singing for the entrance, the antiphon in the Missal is recited either by the faithful, by some of them, or by a reader; otherwise it is recited by the priest after the greeting [GIRM 25–26].

Veneration of the Altar

The priest and ministers must properly venerate the Book of the Gospels (as the word of God, containing the story of Christ) and the altar (as the place the Eucharistic Sacrifice occurs):

> According to the traditional liturgical practice, the altar and the Book of the Gospels are kissed as a sign of veneration. But if this sign of reverence is not in harmony with the traditions of the culture of the region, the conference of bishops may substitute some other sign, after informing the Apostolic See [GIRM 232].

This veneration is to be performed at the end of the entrance procession:

> On reaching the altar the priests and ministers make the proper reverence, that is, a low bow or, if there is a tabernacle containing the Blessed Sacrament, a genuflection.
>
> If the cross has been carried in the procession, it is placed near the altar or at some other convenient place; the candles

carried by the servers are placed near the altar or on a side table; the Book of the Gospels is placed on the altar.

The priest goes up to the altar and kisses it. If incense is used, he incenses the altar while circling it [GIRM 84–85].

If a deacon is present, he also venerates the altar:

With the priest he makes the proper reverence and goes up to the altar. After placing the Book of the Gospels on it, along with the priest he kisses the altar. If incense is used, he assists the priest in putting some in the censer and in incensing the altar [GIRM 129].

Greeting the Congregation

The priest then greets the congregation, and all bless themselves with the sign of the cross:

The priest then goes to the chair. After the entrance song, and with all standing, the priest and the faithful make the sign of the cross. The priest says: *In the name of the Father and of the Son and of the Holy Spirit*; the people answer: *Amen.*

Then, facing the people and with hands outstretched, the priest greets all present, using one of the formularies indicated. He or some other qualified minister may give the faithful a very brief introduction to the Mass of the day [GIRM 86].

Often people ask if it is permitted for the priest or deacon to address the congregation with phrases like "my brothers and sisters," when previously they would have been addressed, "Brethren." The answer is yes. The phrase "my brothers and sisters" appears in the text of one of the optional greetings for the penitential rite, and a rubric footnote to this greeting explains:

At the discretion of the priest, other words that seem more suitable under the circumstances, such as "friends, dearly beloved, brethren," may be used. This also applies to parallel instances in the liturgy.

This kind of text alteration is *not* a liturgical abuse. Neither is the priest personally adapting the greetings and words of conclusion or inserting introductions to specific parts of the Mass:

> It is . . . up to the priest in the exercise of his office of presiding over the assembly to pronounce the instructions and words of introduction and conclusion that are provided in the rites themselves. By their very nature these introductions do not need to be expressed verbatim in the form in which they are given in the Missal; at least in certain cases it will be advisable to adapt them somewhat to the concrete situation of the community. It also belongs to the priest presiding to proclaim the word of God and to give the final blessing. He may give the faithful a very brief introduction to the Mass of the day (before the celebration begins), to the liturgy of the word (before the readings), and to the Eucharistic Prayer (before the preface); he may also make comments concluding the entire sacred service before the dismissal [GIRM 11].

The American *Appendix to the General Instruction* adds to this point:

> With regard to the adaptation of words of introduction, see the circular letter of the Congregation for Divine Worship, April 27, 1973. Number 14 reads:
>
> > Among the possibilities for further accommodating any individual celebration, it is important to consider admonitions, the homily, and the general intercessions. First of all are the admonitions. These enable the people to be drawn into a fuller understanding of the sacred action, or any of

its parts, and lead them into a true spirit of participation. The *General Instruction of the Roman Missal* entrusts the more important admonitions to the priest for preparation and use. He may introduce the Mass to the people before the celebration begins, during the liturgy of the word prior to the actual readings, and the Eucharistic prayer before the preface; he may also conclude the entire sacred action before the dismissal. The *Order of Mass* provides others as well, which are important to certain portions of the rite, such as during the penitential rite, or before the Lord's Prayer. By their very nature these brief admonitions do not require that everyone use them in the form in which they appear in the *Missal*. Provision can be made in certain cases that they be adapted to some degree to the varying circumstances of the community. In all cases it is well to remember the nature of the admonition, and not make them into a sermon or a homily; care should be taken to keep them brief and not too wordy, for otherwise they become tedious [AGI 11].

Penitential Rite

The congregants then reflect on their sins and ask God to forgive them, so that they may be spiritually purified for the celebration of the liturgy:

> After greeting the congregation, the priest or other qualified minister may very briefly introduce the faithful to the Mass of the day. Then the priest invites them to take part in the penitential rite, which the entire community carries out through a communal confession and which the priest's absolution brings to an end [GIRM 29].

It is important to note that this is *not* a sacramental absolution and does not replace going to the sacrament of confession. One who has an unconfessed mortal sin may *not* receive Communion on the basis of the penitential rite.

The *Code of Canon Law* states:

CANON 960

Individual and integral confession and absolution constitute the only ordinary way by which the faithful person who is aware of serious [Latin, *gravis*, or "grave"] sin is reconciled with God and with the Church; only physical or moral impossibility excuses the person from confession of this type, in which case reconciliation can take place in other ways.

Shockingly, in some parishes priests have actually given a general sacramental absolution at the end of the penitential rite. This is *strictly* prohibited. A general sacramental absolution can be given only in highly exceptional circumstances. The *Code of Canon Law* goes on to state:

CANON 961 §1.

Absolution cannot be imparted in a general manner to a number of penitents at once without previous individual confession unless:

1° the danger of death is imminent and there is not time for the priest or priests to hear the confessions of the individual penitents;

2° a serious [Latin, *gravis*] necessity exists, that is, when in light of the number of penitents a supply of confessors is not readily available rightly to hear the confessions of individuals within a suitable time so that the penitents are forced to be deprived of sacramental grace or Holy Communion for a long time through no fault of their own; it is not considered a sufficient necessity if confessors cannot be readily available only because of the great number of penitents as can occur on the occasion of some great feast or pilgrimage.

An example of the kind of situation mentioned in 1° would be a platoon of soldiers about to rush into battle or the passengers in a crashing airplane. An example of the kind of situation mentioned in 2° would be a large group of people on an island or in a remote area who have access to a priest every few months for only long enough to have him say Mass before he has to leave.

In the latter kind of case, however, there is no imminent danger, and an individual priest is not authorized to judge that such a situation exists. Instead, the diocesan bishop must make this determination:

CANON 961 §2

It is for the diocesan bishop to judge whether the conditions required in §1, n. 2, are present; he can determine general cases of such necessity in the light of criteria agreed upon with other members of the conference of bishops.

If a priest were to make an illicit but otherwise valid sacramental absolution, it would have its intended effect so long as the penitent has the required dispositions and intentions:

CANON 962

§1. For a member of the Christian faithful validly to enjoy sacramental absolution given to many at one time, it is required that this person not only be suitably disposed but also at the same time intend to confess individually the serious [Latin, *gravia*, or "grave"] sins which at present cannot be so confessed.

§2. As much as can be done, the Christian faithful are to be instructed concerning the requirements specified in §1, also on the occasion of receiving general absolution; an exhortation that each person take care to make an act of contrition is to precede general absolution, even in danger of death if time is available.

A person who receives a general absolution must then go to regular confession as soon as possible. General absolution *is not* a substitute for individual confession:

CANON 963

With due regard for the obligation mentioned in canon. 989 [i.e., to confess one's grave sins once a year after reaching the age of discretion], a person who has had serious [Latin, *gravia*] sins remitted by a general absolution is to approach individual confession as soon as there is an opportunity to do so before receiving another general absolution unless a just cause intervenes.

Fortunately, priests who are so disobedient or misinformed that they administer a general sacramental absolution at the end of the penitential rite are rare.

If anything, people ask more frequently about the *omission* of the penitential rite at the beginning of a Sunday Mass and whether this is permitted. The answer is that it is supposed to be omitted in some cases. The rubrics for the rite of blessing and sprinkling of holy water state that:

> When this rite is used, it takes the place of the penitential rite at the beginning of Mass. The "Kyrie" is also omitted.

On the other hand, the penitential rite is not simply an optional part of Mass that can be omitted for no cause.

Kyrie Eleison and Gloria

If it has not already been sung or recited, the *Kyrie Eleison* ("Lord have mercy . . .") is then sung:

> Then the *Kyrie* begins, unless it has already been included as part of the penitential rite. Since it is a song by which the faithful praise the Lord and implore his mercy, it is ordinarily prayed by all, that is, alternately by the congregation and the choir or cantor.

As a rule each of the acclamations is said twice, but, because of the idiom of different languages, the music, or other circumstances, it may be said more than twice or a short verse (trope) may be interpolated. If the *Kyrie* is not sung, it is to be recited [GIRM 30].

Following this on most Sundays is the *Gloria* ("Glory to God in the highest, and peace to his people on earth . . ."):

The *Gloria* is an ancient hymn in which the Church, assembled in the Holy Spirit, praises and entreats the Father and the Lamb. It is sung by the congregation, or by the congregation alternately with the choir, or by the choir alone. If not sung, it is to be recited either by all together or in alternation.

The *Gloria* is sung or said on Sundays outside Advent and Lent, on solemnities and feasts, and in special, more solemn celebrations [GIRM 31].

Opening Prayer or Collect

The introductory rites come to a conclusion with the opening prayer:

Next the priest invites the people to pray and together with him they observe a brief silence so that they may realize they are in God's presence and may call their petitions to mind. The priest then says the opening prayer, which custom has named the "collect." This expresses the theme of the celebration and the priest's words address a petition to God the Father through Christ in the Holy Spirit.

The people make the prayer their own and give their assent by the acclamation, *Amen* . . . [GIRM 32].

With the introductory rites accomplished, the liturgy of the word begins.

5. Liturgy of the Word

The *General Instruction* describes the liturgy of the word and its parts in this way:

> Readings from Scripture and the chants between the readings form the main part of the liturgy of the word. The homily, profession of faith, and general intercessions or prayer of the faithful expand and complete this part of the Mass. In the readings, explained by the homily, God is speaking to his people, opening up to them the mystery of redemption and salvation, and nourishing their spirit; Christ is present to the faithful through his own word. Through the chants the people make God's word their own, and through the profession of faith affirm their adherence to it. Finally, having been fed by this word, they make their petitions in the general intercessions for the needs of the Church and for the salvation of the whole world [GIRM 33].

Scripture Readings

WHO MAY DO THE READINGS

The *General Instruction of the Roman Missal* states:

> The reader is instituted to proclaim the readings from Scripture, with the exception of the Gospel. He may also announce the intentions for the general intercessions and, in the absence of the psalmist, sing or read the psalm between the readings.
>
> The reader has his own proper function in the Eucharistic celebration and should exercise this even though ministers of a higher rank may be present.

Those who exercise the ministry of reader, even if they have not received institution, must be truly qualified and carefully prepared in order that the faithful will develop a warm and lively love for Scripture from listening to the reading of the sacred texts [GIRM 66].

Concerning the reading of the Gospel, it states:

The readings lay the table of God's word for the faithful and open up the riches of the Bible to them. Since by tradition the reading of the Scripture is a ministerial, not a presidential, function, it is proper that as a rule a deacon or, in his absence, a priest other than the one presiding read the Gospel. A reader proclaims the other readings. In the absence of a deacon or another priest, the priest celebrant reads the Gospel [GIRM 34].

Regarding the manner in which the gospel reading is to be done, the *General Instruction* states:

At the lectern the priest opens the book and says *The Lord be with you.* Then he says *A reading from . . .* making the sign of the cross with his thumb on the book and on his forehead, mouth, and breast. If incense is used, he then incenses the book. After the acclamation of the people, he proclaims the Gospel and at the end kisses the book, saying inaudibly: *May the words of the Gospel wipe away our sins.* After the reading the people make an acclamation customary to the region [GIRM 95].

Due to the frequent violations, in some areas, of the rule of reserving the Gospel reading to the ordained, *Inaestimabile Donum* was especially firm on the Gospel's reading being reserved to a deacon or priest:

The reading of the Gospel passage is reserved to the ordained minister, namely the deacon or the priest. When possible, the other readings should be entrusted to a reader who has been instituted as such, or to other spiritually and technically trained lay people. The first reading is followed by a responsorial psalm, which is an integral part of the liturgy of the word [ID 2].

The only exceptions to this are on two Sundays of the year. On Palm Sunday (Passion Sunday) the Gospel is read as a dialogue with a priest always taking the part of Christ:

> The passion narrative occupies a special place [in the liturgy of Palm Sunday]. It should be sung or read in the traditional way, that is, by three persons who take the parts of Christ, the narrator, and the people. The passion is proclaimed by deacons or priests, or by lay readers. In the latter case, the part of Christ should be reserved to the priest. . . . For the spiritual good of the faithful, the passion should be proclaimed in its entirety, and the readings which precede it should not be omitted [PS 33].

The same is true of the Gospel on Good Friday (cf. PS 66).

WHICH TRANSLATIONS MAY BE USED

Since the Holy See has reserved to itself the approval of translations of Scripture readings used at Mass (CIC 838 §§2–3, quoted in chapter 1 in the section on who can change the liturgy; cf. CIC 826 §1), only lectionaries approved by the Holy See may be used for the Scripture readings.

At the present time, lectionaries have been approved that are based on the following Bible translations: the 1970 edition of the *New American Bible* (this is the one most commonly used at Masses in America), the *Revised Standard Version: Catholic Edition*, the *Jerusalem Bible*, and the *Contemporary English Version* for children's Masses.

Currently, no lectionaries have been approved that are based on the *Revised New American Bible* (RNAB), the *New Jerusalem Bible* (NJB), or the *New Revised Standard Version* (NRSV). The

Canadian bishops' conference has been given *temporary* permission to use an NRSV Lectionary *in Canada only*.

Helen Hull Hitchcock, a frequent writer on liturgical subjects, explains:

> Many readers have expressed concern about whether the *New Revised Standard Version* of the Bible is permitted for liturgical use. Even after Vatican confirmation of this translation of the Bible was rescinded last year [1994], some people say the NRSV is being used at Mass in their parishes or dioceses.
>
> The confusion over the NRSV is compounded because of a situation in the Canadian Church.
>
> After the letter from Archbishop Geraldo Agnelo, Secretary of the Congregation for Divine Worship, was received by the presidents of English-speaking bishops' conferences last year, the Canadian bishops asked for and received permission from the Holy See for interim use of liturgical books incorporating the NRSV texts they had already printed without proper authorization.
>
> The permission to continue to use these unauthorized books was granted to the *Canadian Church only*, with the understanding that the Canadian bishops would correct the books as soon as possible after the Holy See completes its examination of Scripture translations proposed for liturgical use and authorizes texts for the English-speaking churches.
>
> Catholics in the United States are further confused because some liturgical workbooks printed in the U.S. have included the unauthorized NRSV Lectionary readings printed alongside the authorized readings from the *New American Bible*. The NAB translation was produced for the U.S. Bishops by its official agency, the Confraternity of Christian Doctrine, for use in churches in the United States. This is the version that appears in lectionaries and missalettes [*Adoremus Bulletin*, 1:5 (March 1996); cf. *Origins* 24:22:376f. (November 10, 1994) and 24:24:402 (November 24, 1994)].

At the June 1997 meeting of the U.S. bishops' conference, a motion was considered to approve the first volume of a two-volume lectionary based on the RNAB and NAB. This work was termed the *Lectionary for Mass for use in the Dioceses of the United States of America* (LFM). After absentee ballots had been counted, on August 1, 1997, Bishop Anthony M. Pilla, president of the NCCB, announced that the motion had passed with a vote of 199 to 50. A two-thirds vote of 174 was needed to have the lectionary forwarded to the Holy See for confirmation (NCCB, *Committee on Liturgy Newsletter* [June/July 1997] 33:25).

The first volume of the LFM was approved by the Holy See and now may be used at Mass (see pp. 246–247). At this writing, other approved lectionaries still may be used as well. Changes will be noted in future editions of this book.

Because the Holy See has reserved to itself the approval of Scripture texts in Lectionary form for Mass, it is not permissible for *any individual* to revise these texts, such as doing spontaneous gender revisions to the language of texts that one perceives as "sexist." Tampering with the text of the Sacred Page to fit a modern social-political agenda is a serious liturgical abuse.

As an illustration of how serious the Holy See is about not gender-revising texts, see the appendix on guidelines for translators.

WHICH TEXTS MAY BE USED

The *General Instruction of the Roman Missal* sets out the general guidelines for the number and kind of readings required on Sunday:

> Sundays and holy days have three readings, that is, from the Old Testament, from the writings of an apostle, and from a

Gospel. Thus God's own teaching brings the Christian people to a knowledge of the continuity of the work of salvation.

Accordingly, it is expected that there will be three readings, but for pastoral reasons and by decree of the conference of bishops, the use of only two readings is allowed in some places. In such a case, the choice between the first two readings should be based on the norms in the Lectionary and on the intention to lead the people to a deeper knowledge of Scripture; there should never be any thought of choosing a text because it is shorter or easier [GIRM 318].

It also deals with the kind of readings used at daily Masses during the week:

In the weekday Lectionary, readings are provided for each day of every week throughout the year; therefore, unless a solemnity or feast occurs, these readings are for the most part to be used on the days to which they are assigned.

The continuous reading during the week, however, is sometimes interrupted by the occurrence of a feast or particular celebration. In this case the priest, taking into consideration the entire week's plan of readings, is allowed either to combine omitted parts with other readings or to give preference to certain readings [GIRM 319].

Though a set program of readings is normally required, there are exceptions to this rule:

In Masses with special groups, the priest may choose texts more suited to the particular celebration, provided they are taken from the texts of an approved Lectionary [*ibid.*].

CHANTS BETWEEN THE READINGS

In addition to the reading of Scripture, chanting and singing it has been an important part of Christian liturgy throughout history, and is so today as well, especially in connection with the psalms, which were originally sung in the Jewish liturgy before the time of Christ.

The *General Instruction* states:

> After the first reading comes the responsorial psalm or gradual, an integral part of the liturgy of the word. The psalm as a rule is drawn from the Lectionary because the individual psalm texts are directly connected with the individual readings: The choice of psalm depends therefore on the readings. Nevertheless, in order that the people may be able to join in the responsorial psalm more readily, some texts of responses and psalms have been chosen, according to the different seasons of the year and classes of saints, for optional use, whenever the psalm is sung, in place of the text corresponding to the reading.
>
> The psalmist or cantor of the psalm sings the verses of the psalm at the lectern or other suitable place. The people remain seated and listen, but also as a rule take part by singing the response, except when the psalm is sung straight through without the response.
>
> The psalm when sung may be either the psalm assigned in the Lectionary or the gradual from the *Graduale Romanum* or the responsorial psalm or the psalm with *Alleluia* as the response from the Simple Gradual in the form they have in those books [GIRM 36].

The American *Appendix to the General Instruction* gives additional options:

> As a further alternative . . . the conference of bishops has approved the use of other collections of psalms and antiphons in English, as supplements to the *Simple Gradual*, including psalms arranged in responsorial form, metrical and similar versions of psalms, provided they are used in accordance with the principles of the *Simple Gradual* and are selected in harmony with the liturgical season feast or occasion (decree confirmed by the Consilium for the Implementation of the Constitution on the Liturgy, December 17, 1968).

The choice of texts that are *not* from the Psalter (permitted
at the entrance, offertory and Communion) is not extended to
the chants between the readings . . . [AGI 36].

In most seasons of the liturgical year, an *Alleluia* is sung prior
to the reading of the Gospel:

As the season requires, the *Alleluia* or another chant follows the
second reading.

a. The *Alleluia* is sung in every season outside Lent. It is begun either by all present or by the choir or cantor; it may then
be repeated. The verses are taken from the Lectionary or the
Graduale.

b. The other chant consists of the verse before the Gospel
or another psalm or tract, as found in the Lectionary or the
Graduale [GIRM 37].

Because the *Alleluia* before the Gospel is not permitted during Lent, the American *Appendix* offers the following alterna-
tives:

During Lent the *Alleluia* is not sung with the verse before the
Gospel. Instead one of the following (or similar) acclamations
may be sung before and after the verse before the Gospel:

Praise and honor to you, Lord Jesus Christ, King of endless glory!
Praise and honor to you, Lord Jesus Christ!
Glory and praise to you, Lord Jesus Christ!
Glory to you, Word of God, Lord Jesus Christ!

If the psalm is not sung, it is recited. The *Alleluia* or the verse
before the Gospel may be omitted if not sung (see no. 39 of
the *General Instruction*). The people stand for the singing of the
alleluia before the Gospel (see no. 21 of the *General Instruction*)
[AGI 36].

There are variations in which responses are used during the
psalm. The response that is printed in the missalette is not the
only option:

When there is only one reading before the Gospel:

a. during a season calling for the *Alleluia*, there is an option to use either the psalm with *Alleluia* as the response, or the responsorial psalm and the *Alleluia* with its verse, or just the plain psalm, or just the *Alleluia*;

b. during the season when the Alleluia is not allowed, either the responsorial psalm or the verse before the Gospel may be used [GIRM 38].

The psalm itself, however, is important and belongs in the liturgy even if not accompanied by music or performed by singing. It is different with the Gospel *Alleluia*, which may be omitted if it is not sung:

If the psalm after the reading is not sung, it is to be recited. If not sung, the *Alleluia* or the verse before the Gospel may be omitted [GIRM 39].

Homily

The *General Instruction* states:

The homily is an integral part of the liturgy and is strongly recommended: it is necessary for the nurturing of the Christian life. It should develop some point of the readings or of another text from the Ordinary or from the Proper of the Mass of the day, and take into account the mystery being celebrated and the needs proper to the listeners [GIRM 41].

Inaestimabile Donum clarifies the homily's purpose:

The purpose of the homily is to explain to the faithful the Word of God proclaimed in the readings and to apply its message to the present. Accordingly the homily is to be given by the priest or the deacon [ID 3].

The *Code of Canon Law* is clear that only priests (including bishops) or deacons may give homilies:

CANON 767 §§1–2, 4

Among the forms of preaching, the homily is preeminent; it is a part of the liturgy itself and is reserved to a priest or to a deacon . . .

Whenever a congregation is present a homily is to be given at all Sunday Masses and at Masses celebrated on holy days of obligation; it cannot be omitted without a serious [Latin, *gravi* or "grave"] reason. . . .

It is the duty of the pastor or rector of a church to see to it that these prescriptions are conscientiously observed.

There are, however, limited cases in which a lay person can preach in a church or oratory (CIC 766), but they may not preach the homily during Mass. The Holy See confirmed this in an authentic interpretation of canon 767:

The Doubt: Whether the diocesan bishop is able to dispense from the prescription of canon 767 §1, by which the homily is reserved to priests and deacons.

The Response: Negative [AAS 79 (1987), 1249, cf. DOL 1768].

One cannot circumvent this requirement by omitting the homily and having a lay person give a "faith talk" or something in its place on Sundays and holy days of obligation. At such times, a homily must be given:

There must be a homily on Sundays and holy days of obligation at all Masses that are celebrated with a congregation. It is recommended on other days, especially on the weekdays of Advent, Lent, and the Easter season, as well as on other feasts and occasions when the people come to church in large numbers [GIRM 42].

The Church's seriousness about the reservation of the homily to priests and deacons was again emphasized in the instruction on collaboration:

> The homily, therefore, during the celebration of the Holy Eucharist, must be reserved to the sacred minister-priest or deacon —to the exclusion of the non-ordained faithful, even if these should have responsibilities as "pastoral assistants" or catechists in whatever type of community or group. This exclusion is not based on the preaching ability of sacred ministers nor their theological preparation, but on that function which is reserved to them in virtue of having received the Sacrament of Holy Orders. For the same reason the diocesan Bishop cannot validly dispense from the canonical norm . . . For the same reason, the practice, on some occasions, of entrusting the preaching of the homily to seminarians or theology students who are not clerics is not permitted. Indeed, the homily should not be regarded as a training for some future ministry. . . .
>
> In no instance may the homily be entrusted to priests or deacons who have lost the clerical state or who have abandoned the sacred ministry [ICP, Practical Provisions 3 §1, 5].

The instruction also clarifies the non-homiletic role the laity can play during the Mass:

> A form of instruction designed to promote a greater understanding of the liturgy, including personal testimonies, or the celebration of Eucharistic liturgies on special occasions (e.g., day of the seminary, day of the sick, etc.) is lawful, if in harmony with liturgical norms, [and] should such be considered objectively opportune as a means of explicating the regular homily preached by the celebrant priest. Nonetheless, these testimonies or explanations may not be such so as to assume a character which could be confused with the homily.
>
> As an expositional aide and providing it does not delegate the duty of preaching to others, the celebrant minister may make

prudent use of "dialogue" in the homily, in accord with the
liturgical norms [ibid., 3 §§2, 3].

The instruction does indicate that, theoretically at least, there
are some circumstances in which the laity might be able to
preach homilies, but only in non-Eucharistic liturgies (i.e.,
liturgies which are not Masses or Communion services), and
then only on strict conditions:

> Homilies in non-Eucharistic liturgies may be preached by the
> non-ordained faithful only when expressly permitted by law and
> when its prescriptions for doing so are observed [ibid. 3 §4].

Concerning the location from which the homily is to be
given, the *General Instruction* states:

> The homily is given at the chair or at the lectern [GIRM 97].

In Jesus' day, the customary position from which to teach
was sitting (cf. John 8:2). However, today the homily is normally given standing at the lectern. Both of these practices are
allowed. However, as the directive above shows, the homilist
is not authorized to walk about the sanctuary or even into the
aisle of the nave while giving the homily. This practice is dis-
tracting, and many people find it irritating—especially if the
homilist walks into the nave—for the people in the front rows
may have trouble hearing him and are forced to turn around
in order to look at him while he speaks.

Profession of Faith

After the homily, all profess their faith in God and the chief
truths of Christianity by reciting the profession of faith:

> The symbol or profession of faith [i.e., the creed] in the cele-
> bration of Mass serves as a way for the people to respond and

to give their assent to the word of God heard in the readings and through the homily and for them to call to mind the truths of the faith before they begin to celebrate the Eucharist [GIRM 43].

Without special permission, it is not permitted for a pastor to omit the recitation of the creed on Sundays and solemnities:

Recitation of the profession of faith by the priest together with the people is obligatory on Sundays and solemnities. It may be said also at special, more solemn celebrations [GIRM 44].

The profession of faith that is to be used is the one found in the Sacramentary—that is, the Nicene Creed. It must be used except in children's Masses, for which the rubrics state:

In celebrations of Masses with children, the Apostles' Creed may be said after the homily.

The rubrics note that the Apostles' Creed is

[f]or use only in countries where approved for Mass. It may be said in the U.S. in celebrations of Masses with children.

During the recitation of the Nicene Creed, all make the appropriate sign of reverence at the mention of our Lord's Incarnation:

The profession of faith is said by the priest together with the people. At the words *by the power of the Holy Spirit*, etc., all bow; on the solemnities of the Annunciation and Christmas all kneel [GIRM 98].

Since the Holy See has reserved approval of all liturgical texts to itself (CIC 838 §2, 846 §1), it is not permissible to use alternative creeds, altered versions of the Nicene Creed, or unapproved translations of the Nicene Creed during Mass. For example, it is not permissible to delete the word "men" from "for us men and for our salvation."

General Intercessions

The *General Instruction of the Roman Missal* explains the purpose of the prayer of the faithful, which follows the recitation of the creed:

> In the general intercessions or prayer of the faithful, the people, exercising their priestly function, intercede for all humanity. It is appropriate that this prayer be included in all Masses celebrated with a congregation, so that petitions will be offered for the Church, for civil authorities, for those oppressed by various needs, for all people, and for the salvation of the world [GIRM 45].

This priestly function is an exercise of the common or universal priesthood shared by all the baptized. Saint Peter refers to this priesthood when he tells his readers: "Let yourselves be built into a spiritual house to be a holy priesthood to offer spiritual sacrifices acceptable to God through Jesus Christ. . . . [Y]ou are a chosen race, a royal priesthood, a holy nation" (1 Peter 2:5b, 9). This priesthood is referred to elsewhere in Scripture (cf. Rev. 1:6; cf. Rev. 5:9–10). It is distinct, however, from the ministerial priesthood exercised by the ordained and it does suffice for one to perform the Eucharistic sacrifice. The *Catechism of the Catholic Church* states:

> The ministerial priesthood differs in essence from the common priesthood of the faithful because it confers a sacred power for the service of the faithful. The ordained ministers exercise their service for the People of God by teaching (*munus docendi*), divine worship (*munus liturgicum*), and pastoral governance (*munus regendi*) [CCC 1592].

However, the universal priesthood of the faithful is sufficient for them to intercede with God in prayer, as expressed in the general intercessions in Mass. In most cases there is to be a specific order for the intentions:

> As a rule the sequence of intentions is to be:
>   a. for the needs of the Church;
>   b. for public authorities and the salvation of the world;
>   c. for those oppressed by any need;
>   d. for the local community.
>
> In particular celebrations, such as confirmations, marriages, funerals, etc., the series of intercessions may refer more specifically to the occasion [GIRM 46].

Even in the exercise of the priesthood of the faithful in prayer, the laity are presided over by a ministerial priest, and it is preferred that a deacon announce the intentions:

> It belongs to the priest celebrant to direct the general intercessions, by means of a brief introduction to invite the congregation to pray, and after the intercessions to say the concluding prayer. It is desirable that a deacon, cantor, or other person announce the intentions. The whole assembly gives expression to its supplication either by a response said together after each intention or by silent prayer [GIRM 47].

Typically, the intentions are announced from the lectern, though other places are permitted:

> After the priest introduces the general intercessions, the deacon announces the intentions at the lectern or other suitable place [GIRM 132].

The general intercessions conclude the liturgy of the word, and following them the liturgy of the Eucharist begins.

6. Preparation of the Altar and the Gifts

The liturgy of the Eucharist now begins. This is the central part of the liturgy due to its direct institution by Christ:

> At the Last Supper Christ instituted the sacrifice and paschal meal that make the sacrifice of the cross to be continuously present in the Church, when the priest, representing Christ the Lord, carries out what the Lord did and handed over to his disciples to do in his memory.
>
> Christ took the bread and the cup and gave thanks, saying: "Take and eat, this is my Body." Giving the cup, he said: "Take and drink, this is the cup of my Blood. Do this in memory of me." Accordingly, the Church has planned the celebration of the Eucharistic liturgy around the parts corresponding to these words and actions of Christ:
>
> 1. In the preparation of the gifts, the bread and the wine with water are brought to the altar, that is, the same elements that Christ used.
>
> 2. In the Eucharistic prayer thanks is given to God for the whole work of salvation and the gifts of bread and wine become the Body and Blood of Christ.
>
> 3. Through the breaking of the one bread the unity of the faithful is expressed and through Communion they receive the Lord's Body and Blood in the same way the apostles received them from Christ's own hands [GIRM 48].

In case a deacon is present, his role in the preparation of the altar and gifts is described as follows:

At the presentation of the gifts, while the priest remains at the chair, the deacon prepares the altar, assisted by other ministers, but the care of the sacred vessels belongs to the deacon. He assists the priest in receiving the people's gifts. Next, he hands the priest the paten with bread to be consecrated, pours wine and a little water into the chalice, saying inaudibly the prayer, *Through the mystery of this water and wine*, then passes the chalice to the priest. (He may also prepare the chalice and pour the wine and water at a side table.) If incense is used the deacon assists the priest with the incensing of the gifts and the altar; afterward he, or another minister, incenses the priest and the people [GIRM 133].

Preparation of the Altar

The liturgy of the Eucharist typically begins with a song, during which the articles needed for the celebration of the Eucharist are bought to the altar:

> After the general intercessions, the presentation song begins (see no. 50). The servers place the corporal, purificator, chalice, and missal on the altar [GIRM 100].

The corporal is a square piece of linen. The chalice, paten, and host are placed on it during this part of the Mass. The purificator is a linen cloth used to dry the sacred vessels at the end of or after Mass, that is, when they are purified. The chalice is the vessel used to hold the wine that is consecrated to become the Precious Blood, while a missal, also called a sacramentary, is a book from which the priest reads the prayers of the Mass.

The *General Instruction* notes that there is an exception to placing the chalice on the altar:

> At the beginning of the liturgy of the Eucharist the gifts, which will become Christ's Body and Blood, are bought to the altar.

First the altar, the Lord's table, which is the center of the whole Eucharistic liturgy, is prepared: the corporal, purificator, missal, and chalice are placed on it (unless the chalice is prepared at a side table) [GIRM 49].

Thus it is not an abuse for the priest to prepare the chalice on a side table rather than on the altar.

Presentation of the Elements and Offerings

Also at this time, the elements—the bread and wine that will be consecrated—are presented:

The gifts are then brought forward. It is desirable for the faithful to present the bread and wine, which are accepted by the priest or deacon at a convenient place . . . . Even though the faithful no longer, as in the past, bring the bread and wine for the liturgy from their homes, the rite of carrying up the gifts retains the same spiritual value and meaning [GIRM 49].

Concerning the amount of the elements that are to be brought forward, the rubrics in the Sacramentary state:

Sufficient hosts (and wine) for the Communion of the faithful are to be prepared. It is most important that the faithful should receive the Body of the Lord in hosts consecrated at the same Mass and should share the cup when it is permitted. Communion is thus a clearer sign of sharing in the sacrifice which is actually taking place.

For information on the kind of hosts and wine that are to be used, see chapter 3.

At the same time that the elements to be consecrated are brought forward, it is also typical to receive other offerings. These are usually from a collection that has just been taken up:

This is also the time to receive money or other gifts for the Church or the poor brought by the faithful or collected at Mass. These are to be put in a suitable place but not on the altar [GIRM 49].

Note the altar is *not* an acceptable location for the faithful's monetary offerings to be placed. It is not proper for a priest or minister to put a collection basket on the altar.

All of this activity is covered by the presentation song, which does not end until the gifts have been received and the elements placed on the altar:

> The procession bringing the gifts is accompanied by the presentation song, which continues at least until the gifts have been placed on the altar. The rules for the song are the same as those for the entrance song [cf. GIRM 26]. If it is not sung, the presentation antiphon is omitted [GIRM 50].

Preparation of the Elements

Once the elements to be consecrated have been received, they may be incensed:

> The gifts on the altar and the altar itself may be incensed. This is a symbol of the Church's offering and prayer going up to God. Afterward the deacon or other minister may incense the priest and the people [GIRM 51].

Even after the gifts are received, there are rites to be performed over the elements.

> At the altar the priest receives the paten with the bread from a minister. With both hands he holds it slightly raised above the altar and says the accompanying prayer. Then he places the paten with the bread on the corporal [GIRM 102].

The rubrics in the Sacramentary reveal what the priest is supposed to do at this point:

> The priest, standing at the altar, takes the paten with the bread and, holding it slightly raised above the altar, says inaudibly:
>
> *Blessed are you, Lord, God of all creation. Through your goodness we have this bread to offer, which earth has given and human hands have made. It will become for us the bread of life.*
>
> Then he places the paten with the bread on the corporal.
> If no offertory song is sung, the priest may say the preceding words in an audible voice; then the people may respond:
>
> *Blessed be God for ever.*

There is significant flexibility in the above. If there is an offertory song being sung, the priest is supposed to say the prayer inaudibly (that is, very quietly). However, if no song is sung then he has the *option* of saying them loudly enough to be heard, in which case the people have the *option* of responding "Blessed be God for ever." Thus it is not a liturgical abuse for the priest to say the words inaudibly even if there is no song, nor is it an abuse for the people to not respond. If the priest is not saying the words in an audible voice, the people do not need to strain to hear when he finishes so that they can respond. In fact, the rubrics do not even hint that they respond if he says the prayer inaudibly.

> Next, as the minister presents the cruets, the priest stands at the side of the altar and pours a little water into the chalice, saying the accompanying prayer softly. He returns to the middle of the altar, takes the chalice, raises it a little with both hands, and says the appointed prayer. Then he places the chalice on the corporal and may cover it with a pall [GIRM 103].

The deacon or priest then begins the preparation of the wine by pouring a little water into it. The rubrics state:

The deacon (or the priest) pours wine and a little water into the chalice, saying inaudibly:

By the mystery of this water and wine may we come to share in the divinity of Christ, who humbled himself to share in our humanity.

Concerning the amount of water to be mixed with the wine, sacramental theologian Fr. Nicholas Halligan explains:

It is a serious precept which requires that a very small portion of water be mixed with the wine when about to be used in the Holy Sacrifice. This is not necessary by reason of the sacrament but by ecclesiastical precept in order to signify that both water and Blood issued from the side of the crucified Savior [John 19:34]. . . . The quantity to be added is usually three to ten drops. Priests should avoid too great concern over the exact number of drops. Even a single drop, so long as it is sensible, satisfies the precept; even one fifth water (or one fourth if the wine is stronger) is not unlawful, although an excess of one third the amount of wine renders the latter invalid or truly doubtful. If the quantity of water added appears to be more than lawful, the minister should add more wine or take fresh wine and add the correct amount of water [*The Sacraments and Their Celebration* (New York: Alba House, 1986), 67].

Then the priest prays over the chalice. According to the rubrics:

Then the priest takes the chalice, and holding it slightly raised above the altar, says inaudibly:

Blessed are you, Lord, God of all creation. Through your goodness we have this wine to offer, fruit of the vine and work of human hands. It will become our spiritual drink.

Then he places the chalice on the corporal.

If no offertory song is sung, the priest may say the preceding words in an audible voice; then the people may respond:

Blessed be God for ever.

This has the same flexibility concerning whether it is said audibly or inaudibly and whether the people respond as does the corresponding prayer over the bread. Also, like the corresponding prayer, there is no set height to which the priest is supposed to elevate the chalice (or in the case of the preceding prayer, the paten). He is merely directed to raise it slightly above the corporal.

One way in which the prayers over the bread and the wine *do not have flexibility* concerns a practice that is reported in some areas of a priest holding *both* the paten and the chalice above the corporal and fusing the two prayers together, along these lines:

> Blessed are you, Lord, God of all creation. Through your goodness we have this bread and wine to offer . . .

This is contrary to the rubrics and requires the priest to *ad lib* in an attempt to fuse the disparate parts of the two prayers. It is not allowed.

The rubrics then state:

> The priest bows and says inaudibly:
>
> Lord God, we ask you to receive us and be pleased with the sacrifice we offer you with humble and contrite hearts.
>
> He may then incense the offering and the altar. Afterwards the deacon or a minister incenses the people.

Lavabo *or Rite of Hand Washing*

Afterwards comes a rite known as the *lavabo:*

> The priest then washes his hands as an expression of his desire to be cleansed within [GIRM 52].

He typically washes his hands while a minister pours water over them:

After the prayer, *Lord God, we ask you to receive,* or after the incensation, the priest washes his hands at the side of the altar and inaudibly says the prescribed prayer as a minister pours the water [GIRM 106].

The Sacramentary indicates that the prescribed prayer at this point is:

"Lord, wash away my iniquity; cleanse me from my sin."

The Holy See has called particular attention to the *lavabo* or rite of the priest washing his hands during Mass:

Query: May the rite of washing the hands be omitted from the celebration of Mass?

Reply: In no way.

Both the GIRM (nos. 52, 106, 222) and the Order of Mass (with a congregation, no. 24; without a congregation, no. 18) show the *lavabo* to be one of the prescribed rites in the preparation of the gifts. A rite of major importance is clearly not at issue, but it is not to be dropped since its meaning is: "an expression of the (priest's) desire to be cleansed within" (GIRM 52). In the course of the Consilium's work on the Order of Mass, there were a number of debates on the value and the place to be assigned to the *lavabo*, e.g., on whether it should be a rite in silence or with an accompanying text; there was, however, unanimity that it must be retained. Even though there has been no practical reason for the act of handwashing since the beginning of the Middle Ages, its symbolism is obvious and understood by all (see SC 34). The rite is a usage in all liturgies of the West.

The Constitution on the Liturgy (SC 37–40) envisions ritual adaptations to be suggested by the conferences of bishops and submitted to the Holy See. Such adaptations must be based on serious reasons, for example, the specific culture and viewpoint of a people, contrary and unchangeable usages, the practical impossibility of adapting some new rite that is foreign to the genus of a people, and so on.

Apart from the envisioned exemptions from rubrics and differing translations of texts (see *Consilium, Instr.* 25 Jan. 1969), the Order of Mass is presented as a single unit whose general structure and individual components must be exactly respected. Arbitrary selectiveness on the part of an individual or a community would soon result in the ruin of a patiently and thoughtfully constructed work [*Notitiae* 6 (1970) 38–39, no. 27, DOL 1442 n. R12].

Final Prayer over the Gifts

Following the *lavabo*, the priest directs the people to pray. The rubrics of the Mass state:

Standing at the center of the altar, facing the people, he [the priest] extends and then joins his hands, saying:

Pray, brethren, that our sacrifice may be acceptable to God, the Almighty Father.

The people respond:

May the Lord accept the sacrifice at your hands for the praise and glory of his name, for our good and the good of all his Church.

This prayer concludes the preparation of the gifts:

[T]he preparation of the gifts comes to an end through the invitation to pray with the priest and the prayer over the gifts, which are a preparation for the Eucharistic prayer [GIRM 53].

There is also some flexibility in the priest's invitation for the faithful to pray. A rubric footnote states concerning the expression "Pray, brethren," that

At the discretion of the priest, other words which seem more suitable under the circumstances, such as friends, dearly beloved, my brothers and sisters, may be used.

7. Eucharistic Prayer

The focus of the liturgy of the Eucharist is, of course, on the Eucharist itself, in which Christ becomes really present under the appearances of bread and wine—a miracle that the Church refers to as *transubstantiation* and which is still the teaching of the Church today. The *General Instruction of the Roman Missal* states:

> The celebration of Mass also proclaims the sublime mystery of the Lord's Real Presence under the Eucharistic elements, which Vatican Council II and other documents of the Church's Magisterium have reaffirmed in the same sense and as the same teaching that the Council of Trent had proposed as a matter of faith [i.e., infallibly defined]. The Mass does this not only by means of the very words of consecration, by which Christ becomes present through transubstantiation, but also by the spirit and expression of reverence and adoration in which the Eucharistic liturgy is carried out. For the same reason the Christian people are invited in Holy Week on Holy Thursday and on the solemnity of Corpus Christi to honor this wonderful sacrament in a special way by their adoration [GIRM Introduction, 3].

It is because of the transubstantiation that occurs and because of the accompanying Eucharistic Sacrifice that the Mass is so important in the Christian life. This is stressed by the *Code of Canon Law:*

CANON 897

The Most Holy Eucharist is the most august sacrament, in which Christ the Lord himself is contained, offered, and received, and by which the Church constantly lives and grows. The Eucharistic Sacrifice, the memorial of the death and resurrection of the Lord, in which the sacrifice of the cross is perpetuated over the centuries, is the summit and the source of all Christian worship and life; it signifies and effects the unity of the people of God and achieves the building up of the Body of Christ. The other sacraments and all the ecclesiastical works of the apostolate are closely related to the Holy Eucharist and are directed to it.

CANON 898

The faithful are to hold the Eucharist in highest honor, taking part in the celebration of the most august Sacrifice, receiving the sacrament devoutly and frequently, and worshiping it with supreme adoration; pastors, clarifying the doctrine on this sacrament, are to instruct the faithful thoroughly about this obligation.

The transubstantiation of the elements and the Eucharistic sacrifice are accomplished in the Eucharistic prayer, which makes it the central point of the liturgy. The *General Instruction* states:

Now the center and summit of the entire celebration begins: the Eucharistic prayer, a prayer of thanksgiving and sanctification. The priest invites the people to lift up their hearts to the Lord in prayer and thanks; he unites them with himself in the prayer he addresses in their name to the Father through Jesus Christ. The meaning of the prayer is that the entire congregation joins itself to Christ in acknowledging the great things God has done and in offering the sacrifice [GIRM 54].

Because of its importance, the Eucharistic prayer must be recited with great care and only by those authorized to do it.

Who May Say the Eucharistic Prayer

The Eucharistic prayer is reserved to the priest:

> It is reserved to the priest, by virtue of his ordination, to proclaim the Eucharistic Prayer, which of its nature is the high point of the whole celebration. It is therefore an abuse to have some parts of the Eucharistic Prayer said by the deacon, by a lower minister, or by the faithful [ID 4].

This does not mean that the faithful are merely spectators during the Eucharistic Prayer:

> On the other hand the assembly does not remain passive and inert; it unites itself to the priest in faith and silence and shows its concurrence by the various interventions provided for in the course of the Eucharistic Prayer: the responses to the Preface dialogue, the *Sanctus* ["Holy, Holy, Holy . . ."], the acclamation after the Consecration [the "Mystery of Faith"], and the final Amen after the *Per Ipsum*. The *Per Ipsum* itself ["Through him, with him, in him . . ."] is reserved to the priest. This Amen especially should be emphasized by being sung, since it is the most important in the whole Mass [*ibid.*].

The *General Instruction* also specifies the appropriate role of the faithful during the Eucharistic prayer:

> The Eucharistic prayer calls for all to listen in silent reverence, but also to take part through the acclamations for which the rite makes provision [GIRM 55].

If a deacon is present, the *General Instruction* is specific about where he is to stand and what he is to do during the Eucharistic prayer.

> During the Eucharistic prayer, the deacon stands near, but slightly behind the priest, so that when necessary he may assist the priest with the chalice or the missal [GIRM 134].

Which Eucharistic Prayers May Be Used

The Church is very strict about which Eucharistic Prayers may be used, due to the possibility of scandal being given if something erroneous or infelicitous were said during the Eucharistic Prayer. As a result,

> Only the Eucharistic Prayers included in the Roman Missal or those that the Apostolic See has by law admitted, in the manner and within the limits laid down by the Holy See, are to be used. To modify the Eucharistic Prayers approved by the Church or to adopt others privately composed is a most serious abuse [ID 5].

Currently, ten Eucharistic Prayers are approved for use in the United States:

 a) the Eucharistic Prayers I (Roman Canon), II, III, IV,
 b) the Eucharistic Prayers for Masses with children I, II, III,
 c) the Eucharistic Prayers for Masses of reconciliation I and II, and
 d) the Eucharistic Prayer for Masses for various needs and occasions (also called the Swiss Synod Eucharistic Prayer).

The Swiss Synod Eucharistic Prayer was approved by the United States NCCB in 1994 and confirmed on May 9, 1995, in a letter to Cardinal William Keeler (then-president of the NCCB). The letter was sent by Cardinal Antonio Javierre (former prefect of the Sacred Congregation for Divine Worship and the Discipline of the Sacraments), and it approved the prayer for temporary use in the United States. Copies of the Swiss Synod Eucharistic Prayer and the letters authorizing its use may be found in a booklet titled *Eucharistic Prayer for Masses for Various Needs and Occasions* (New Jersey: Catholic Book Publishing Co., 1996). It should be noted that this prayer has four variants that appear in the intercessions following the *anamnesis*.

However, the traditional canon of the Latin Rite, Eucharistic Prayer I or the Roman Canon, also has variants for special occasions.

Eucharistic Prayers Approved for Use in the U.S.

To help you recognize the approved Eucharistic prayers, here are the opening lines of each (these occur right after the *Sanctus* or "Holy, Holy, Holy," see below):

STANDARD EUCHARISTIC PRAYERS

   I. "We come to you, Father, with praise and thanksgiving . . ."

   II. "Lord, you are holy indeed, the fountain of all holiness . . ."

   III. "Father, you are holy indeed, and all creation rightly gives you praise . . ."

   IV. "Father, we acknowledge your greatness: all your actions show your wisdom and love . . ."

PRAYERS FOR CHILDREN'S MASSES

   I. "God our Father, you are most holy and we want to show you that we are grateful . . ."

   II. "Blessed be Jesus, whom you sent to be the friend of children and of the poor . . ."

   III. "Yes, Lord, you are holy; you are kind to us and to all . . ."

PRAYERS FOR RECONCILIATION MASSES

   I. "Father, from the beginning of time you have always done what is good for man . . ."

   II. "God of power and might, we praise you through your Son, Jesus Christ . . ."

Swiss Synod Eucharistic Prayer

"You are truly blessed, O God of holiness: You accompany us with love as we journey through life . . ."

Order of the Eucharistic Prayer and Accompanying Actions

Introductory Prayer

The Eucharistic prayer opens with the priest appealing to the people to elevate their hearts to the worship of God:

The priest then begins the Eucharistic prayer. With outstretched hands, he says: *The Lord be with you.* As he says: *Lift up your hearts,* he raises his hands; with hands outstretched, he adds: *Let us give thanks to the Lord our God.* When the people have answered: *It is right to give him thanks and praise,* the priest continues the preface. . . . [GIRM 108].

Preface

The preface that is used with the Eucharistic prayer varies depending on the day and/or the Eucharistic prayer that has been selected. See a copy of the Sacramentary for the text of the approved prefaces and the circumstances in which individual ones are to be used.

One of the key elements expressed in the preface is thanksgiving to God. The *General Instruction* lists it as one of the chief elements of the Eucharistic prayer:

Thanksgiving (expressed especially in the preface): In the name of the entire people of God, the priest praises the Father and gives thanks to him for the whole work of salvation or for some special aspect of it that corresponds to the day, feast, or season [GIRM 55a].

ACCLAMATION OR *SANCTUS*

Following the preface, the priest and the people make the acclamation by singing or saying the *Sanctus* (also known as the *Trisagion* or "Holy, Holy, Holy . . ."). This is considered a principal part of the Eucharistic prayer:

> Acclamation: Joining with the angels, the congregation sings or recites the *Sanctus*. This acclamation is an intrinsic part of the Eucharistic prayer and all the people join with the priest in singing or reciting it [GIRM 55b].

EPICLESIS

The *Epiclesis*, or invocation of God to send the Holy Spirit to transform the elements into the Body and Blood of Christ, is also a key part of the Eucharistic prayer:

> Epiclesis: In special invocations the Church calls on God's power and asks that the gifts offered by human hands be consecrated, that is, become Christ's Body and Blood, and that the victim to be received in Communion be the source of salvation for all those who will partake [GIRM 55c].

RINGING A BELL

Many people ask whether the ringing of a bell during key portions of the Mass is required or permitted or not permitted. GIRM states the following:

> A little before the consecration, the server may ring a bell as a signal to the faithful. Depending on local custom, he also rings

the bell at the showing of both the host and the chalice [GIRM 109].

Later, the Holy See further explained this:

Query: Is a bell to be rung at Mass?

Reply: It all depends on the different circumstances of places and people, as is clear from GIRM 109: "A little before the consecration, the server may ring a bell as a signal to the faithful. Depending on local custom, he also rings the bell at the showing of both the host and the chalice." From a long and attentive catechesis and education in liturgy, a particular liturgical assembly may be able to take part in the Mass with such attention and awareness that it has no need of this signal at the central part of the Mass. This may easily be the case, for example, with religious communities or with particular or small groups. The opposite may be presumed in a parish or public church, where there is a different level of liturgical and religious education and where often people who are visitors or are not regular churchgoers take part. In these cases the bell as a signal is entirely appropriate and is sometimes necessary. To conclude: usually a signal with the bell should be given, at least at the two elevations, in order to elicit joy and attention [*Notitiae* 8 (1972) 343, DOL 1499 n. R28].

INSTITUTION NARRATIVE AND CONSECRATION

Now comes the portion of the Eucharistic prayer in which the elements are consecrated and transformed into the Body and Blood of Christ. The *General Instruction* describes this portion of the Mass as follows:

Institution narrative and consecration: In the words and actions of Christ, that sacrifice is celebrated which he himself instituted at the Last Supper, when, under the appearances of bread and wine, he offered his Body and Blood, gave them to his apostles to eat and drink, then commanded that they carry on this mystery [GIRM 55d].

Words of Consecration

It is gravely *illicit* (not permitted) to use any formula for consecration other than one printed in a translation of the rite of Mass that has been confirmed by the Holy See. If the degree of departure is substantial enough, the consecration will be rendered *invalid* (meaning the elements will not become the Body and Blood of Christ).

Currently there is only one English translation of the words of consecration over the host that has been confirmed by the Holy See:

> *Take this, all of you, and eat it:*
> *This is my Body, which will be given up for you.*

There are, however, two approved English translations of the words of consecration over the chalice that the Holy See has confirmed. The first one—which is used in the four standard Eucharistic Prayers, the two Eucharistic Prayers for Masses of Reconciliation, and the variants of the Swiss Synod Eucharistic Prayer—is this:

> *Take this, all of you, and drink from it:*
> *This is the cup of my Blood,*
> *The Blood of the new and everlasting covenant.*
> *It will be shed for you and for all*
> *So that sins may be forgiven.*
> *Do this in memory of me.*

The formula that has been confirmed for use in the Eucharistic Prayers for Masses with Children, however, contains an additional, clarifying phrase—"Then he said to them"—so the prayer reads:

Take this, all of you, and drink from it:
This is the cup of my Blood,
The Blood of the new and everlasting covenant.
It will be shed for you and for all
So that sins may be forgiven.
Then he said to them:
Do this in memory of me.

This variation does nothing to affect the validity of the consecration nor, since the Holy See has confirmed it, does it affect the liceity. It is not a liturgical abuse for a priest to use this formula of words during children's Masses.

Throughout Christian history, and today in the Eastern Rites of the Catholic Church, a number of formulas have been used and are used in the consecration. Regarding the formulas and what is needed for validity, Fr. Halligan explains,

> The [standard Roman Rite] formula of consecration of the bread is: "This is my Body which will be given up for you"; of the wine: "This is the cup of my Blood, the Blood of the new and everlasting Covenant. It will be shed for you and for all so that sins may be forgiven." The words which precede these formulas in no way pertain to the validity of the formula. It is commonly taught today that the essential words of the formula of the Eucharist—and their omission would invalidate the form—are: "This is my Body," "This is the cup of my Blood" (or "this is my Blood"). In practice it is seriously prescribed to pronounce the entire formula; if any of the words from "the Blood of the new . . . " on are omitted, the whole formula is to be repeated conditionally [*op. cit.,* 67].

Three further points should be made with regard to the words of consecration, as these points are often raised by radical traditionalists.

"For You and for Many"

First, the English translation of the words of consecration over the cup as "It will be shed for you and for all so that sins may be forgiven" is sometimes faulted on the grounds that it is not a fully literal translation of the Latin in this passage. The phrase rendered "for all" (*pro multis* in Latin) would more literally be translated "for the multitudes" or "for many." This is true. However, neither the validity nor the liceity of the English translation is in question.

Here is the Holy See's response concerning this translation:

> In certain vernacular versions of the text for consecrating the wine, the words *pro multis* are translated thus: English, *for all*; Spanish, *por todos*; Italian, *per tutti*.

Query:

a. Is there a sufficient reason for introducing this variant and if so, what is it?

b. Is the pertinent traditional teaching in the Catechism of the Council of Trent to be considered superseded?

c. Are all other versions of the biblical passage in question to be regarded as less accurate?

d. Did something inaccurate and needing correction or emendation in fact slip in when the approval was given for such a version?

Reply: The variant involved is fully justified:

a. According to exegetes the Aramaic word translated in Latin by *pro multis* has as its meaning "for all": the many for whom Christ died is without limit; it is equivalent to saying "Christ has died for all." The words of Saint Augustine are apposite: "See what he gave and you will discover what he bought. The price is Christ's Blood. What is it worth but the whole world? What, but all peoples? Those who say either that the price is so small that it has purchased only Africans are ungrateful for the price they cost; those who say that they are

so important that it has been given for them alone are proud"
[*Enarr. in Ps. 95*, 5].

b. The teaching of the Catechism is in no way superseded: the distinction that Christ's death is sufficient for all but efficacious for many remains valid.

c. In the approval of this vernacular variant in the liturgical text nothing inaccurate has slipped in that requires correction or emendation [*Notitiae* 6 (1970) 39–40, no. 28, DOL 1445 n. R13].

The validity of the consecration if the formula "for all" is used is not in question since it is theologically *true* that Christ shed his blood for all men (1 Tim. 4:10, 1 John 2:2). The claim that he shed his blood only for the elect or only for the faithful was condemned during the Jansenist controversy (D 1096, 1294 [DS 2005, 2304]; cf. CCC 605f). Finally, in biblical idiom, the term "many" is often used as a synonym for "all." For example, when Paul says that "by one man's [Adam's] disobedience *many* were made sinners" (Rom. 5:19), he means that *all* men were made sinners.

The liceity of the translation "for all" is not in question because it is part of a Church-approved text of the Mass.

Mysterium fidei

Second, radical traditionalists are also troubled by the absence of the words *mysterium fidei* ("mystery of faith"), which used to be in the words of consecration over the cup. However, Josef Jungmann, S.J., probably the definitive historian of the Mass, points out in his landmark work that the words *mysterium fidei* are an insertion into the words of consecration that is not original and was made at a later date (*The Mass of the Roman Rite* 2:199–201).

Not only are the words *mysterium fidei* not original in the Mass of the Roman Rite, they have never been and are not now in the Eucharistic Prayers of the Eastern Rites in union with the pope. Yet the Church has always recognized the validity of these Eucharistic Prayers, illustrating that the words *mysterium fidei* are not necessary for validity.

The fact is that, although in the Roman Rite there is only one *licit* form of the words of consecration that may be used, there is no single *valid* formula. The New Testament presents us with four different accounts (Matt. 26:26–28, Mark 14:22–24, Luke 22:19–20, and 1 Cor. 11:24–25), the Eastern Rites of the Church have used and still use different formulas, and even the words in the Latin Rite's version have changed over time.

Intention of the Priest

Third, the intention of the minister in saying the words of consecration is sometimes questioned. What if, for example, the priest did not have the intention for transubstantiation to occur? It is not necessary for the priest to have the *specific* intention that transubstantiation take place, so long as he has the *general* intention to celebrate the sacrament of the Eucharist. Ludwig Ott, in his *Fundamentals of Catholic Dogma* (Rockford, Illinois: TAN, 1974), states that regarding the sacraments:

> Objectively considered, the intention of doing what the Church does suffices. The minister, therefore, does not need to intend what the Church intends, namely to produce the effects of the sacraments, for example, the forgiveness of sins; neither does he need to intend to execute a specific Catholic rite. It suffices if he has the intention of performing the religious action as it is current among Christians [344].

Eucharistic Sacrifice

One question that commonly arises, since the text of the Mass and its supporting guidelines—such as those found in the *General Instruction*—lay so much stress on the sacrificial aspect of the Eucharist, is when the sacrifice itself occurs.

The common teaching is that it is the *transubstantiation* of the two elements that accomplishes the Eucharistic sacrifice (Ott, 409). The consecration of the elements is twofold: First the bread is consecrated, then the wine. Even though Christ's Body and Blood (and soul and divinity) are present under both forms, the two forms depict his Body and Blood in a state of separation, as they were when sacrificed on the cross. Thus it is commonly taught:

> The external sacrifice consists in the sacramental (*mystica*) separation of the Body and Blood of Christ, which is consummated *via verborum* [by force of words] by the double consecration and which is an objective representation (*repraesentatio*) of the historical, real separation consummated on the cross [Ott, 410].

This is also the teaching of Saint Thomas Aquinas, who states that "the opportunity of offering sacrifice is considered . . . chiefly with regard to God, to whom the sacrifice of this sacrament is offered *by consecrating*. . . . [T]his sacrament is performed in the consecration of the Eucharist, *whereby a sacrifice is offered* to God" (*Summa Theologiae* III:82:10, emphasis added).

PRESENTATION OF THE HOST TO THE PEOPLE

Sometimes the faithful are puzzled when different priests elevate the Host or the chalice to different degrees, some scarcely elevating it at all at the consecration. However, the Mass rubrics specify only that after the consecration the priest *show* the consecrated elements to the faithful. He may even turn around to face the congregation and show the sacred species, if he is celebrating Mass without facing the people.

Immediately after the words of consecration of the host, the rubrics for the priest specify:

> He shows the consecrated Host to the people, places it on the paten, and genuflects in adoration.

And immediately after the words of consecration for the chalice, the rubrics specify:

> He shows the chalice to the people, places it on the corporal, and genuflects in adoration.

No specific amount of elevation is mandated at this point. What *is* mandated is that the consecrated elements be *shown* to the faithful for their adoration. Failure to *elevate* them is not a liturgical abuse.

Elevation of the sacred species is mandated, however, at the *Per Ipsum* (see below).

Memorial Acclamation or *"Mystery of Faith"*

After the chalice has been shown to the people, the rubrics in the Sacramentary specify:

> Then he [the priest] sings or says:
>
> *Let us proclaim the mystery of faith:*
>
> People with celebrant and concelebrants:
>
> *Christ has died, Christ is risen, Christ will come again.*

In some places deacons rather than priests have said the line "Let us proclaim the mystery of faith." However, this is not allowed. On January 14, 1983, the Sacred Congregation for the Sacraments and Divine Worship issued a reply to the question of whether deacons could perform this function, and the answer was no:

> The Vicar General of the Diocese of Green Bay (Wisconsin, U.S.A.) asked the Sacred Congregation for the Sacraments and Divine Worship if deacons may announce the "Mystery of Faith" at Mass, which seems to be a custom in [the] U.S.A.
>
> Reply. I am writing with reference to your letter of the 29 September, 1982, concerning the acclamation "MYSTERIUM FIDEI" and the possibility of allocating this acclamation to the deacon. This question has already been carefully studied and, therefore, the prescription of the *Missale Romanum*: "*Deinde (sacerdos) dicit: Mysterium fidei*" (*Ordo Missae*, n. 93) is to be observed (cf. also apostolic constitution, *Missale Romanum* of His Holiness, Pope Paul VI, of the 3 April, 1969).
>
> (Private); S. C. Sacr. et Cult. Div., reply, 14 Jan., 1983, Prot. N. CD 1005/82; original English text; copy kindly sent to C.L.D. by the Office of the U.S. Apostolic delegate.

This reply appeared in *Canon Law Digest* (Mundelein, Illinois: 1986) 10:4.

ANAMNESIS

After the memorial acclamation, the *Anamnesis* or "Remembrance" is said:

> Anamnesis: In fulfillment of the command received from Christ through the apostles, the Church keeps his memorial by recalling especially his passion, resurrection, and ascension [GIRM 55e].

OFFERING

The *Anamnesis* is followed by the offering of Christ and his faithful to the Father:

> Offering: in this memorial, the Church—and in particular the church here and now assembled—offers the spotless victim to the Father in the Holy Spirit. The Church's intention is that the faithful not only offer this victim but also learn to offer themselves and so to surrender themselves, through Christ the Mediator, to an ever more complete union with the Father and with each other, so that at last God may be all in all [GIRM 55f].

INTERCESSIONS

The priest then intercedes with the Father that the fruit of the Eucharist may be applied to varying groups:

> Intercessions: the intercessions make it clear that the Eucharist is celebrated in communion with the entire Church of heaven and earth and that the offering is made for the Church and for all its members, living and dead, who are called to share in the salvation and redemption purchased by Christ's Body and Blood [GIRM 55g].

Included in the intercessions are references to the local bishop, who may have one or more auxiliaries, and these may require special adaptations to be made:

> If the priest celebrant is a bishop, after the words *N. our Pope* or the equivalent, he adds: *and for me your unworthy servant.* The local Ordinary must be mentioned in this way: *N. our Bishop* (or *Vicar, Prelate, Prefect, Abbot*). Coadjutor and auxiliary bishops may be mentioned in the Eucharistic prayer. When several are named, this is done with the collect formula, *N. our Bishop*

and his assistant bishops. All these phrases should be modified grammatically to fit with each one of the Eucharistic prayers [GIRM 109].

FINAL DOXOLOGY OR *PER IPSUM*

The Eucharistic prayer concludes with the final doxology, also known as the *Per Ipsum* (from its opening words in Latin: "Through him . . . "):

> Final doxology: The praise of God is expressed in the doxology, to which the people's acclamation is an assent and a conclusion [GIRM 55h].

At this point, the rubrics do mandate that the Eucharist be elevated:

> He [the priest] takes the chalice and the paten with the host and, lifting them up, sings or says:
>
> *Through him, with him, in him, in the unity of the Holy Spirit, all glory and honor is yours, almighty Father, for ever and ever.*
>
> The people respond: *Amen.*

If a deacon is present, he assists the priest by holding the chalice during the *Per Ipsum*:

> At the final doxology of the Eucharistic prayer, the deacon stands next to the priest, holding up the chalice as the priest raises the paten with the Eucharistic bread, until the people have said the acclamation: *Amen* [GIRM 135].

People thus do not need to worry if they see a deacon doing this. It is not a liturgical abuse.

The *Amen* at the end of the *Per Ipsum* is one of the key moments of the faithful's participation in the Eucharistic prayer, though they are not to say the *Per Ipsum* itself:

[T]he assembly does not remain passive and inert; it unites it-self to the priest in faith and silence and shows its concurrence by the various interventions provided for in the course of the Eucharistic Prayer: the responses to the Preface dialogue, the *Sanctus*, the acclamation after the Consecration, and the final *Amen* after the *Per Ipsum*. The *Per Ipsum* itself is reserved to the priest. This *Amen* especially should be emphasized by being sung, since it is the most important in the whole Mass [ID 4].

The reservation of the *Per Ipsum* to the priest was also stressed in the recent instruction on collaboration:

To promote the proper identity (of various roles) in this area, those abuses which are contrary to the provisions of canon 907 are to be eradicated. In Eucharistic celebrations deacons and non-ordained members of the faithful may not pronounce prayers —e.g., especially the Eucharistic prayer, with its concluding doxology [i.e., the *Per Ipsum*]—or any other parts of the liturgy reserved to the celebrant priest [ICP, Practical Provisions 6 §2].

8. Communion Rite

In the Communion rite that follows the Eucharistic prayer, the faithful receive the Body, Blood, soul, and divinity of Jesus Christ, made truly present under the appearances of bread and wine. For this reason, the Communion rite has great importance:

> Since the Eucharistic celebration is the paschal meal, it is right that the faithful who are properly disposed receive the Lord's Body and Blood as spiritual food as he commanded. This is the purpose of the breaking of bread and the other preparatory rites that lead directly to the Communion of the people [GIRM 56].

It is also preferable that the faithful receive Hosts consecrated during the Mass they are attending and that they partake of both the Host and the chalice when permitted:

> It is most desirable that the faithful receive the Lord's Body from hosts consecrated at the same Mass and that, in the instances when it is permitted, they share in the chalice. Then even through the signs Communion will stand out more clearly as a sharing in the sacrifice actually being celebrated [GIRM 56h].

Who May Give and Receive Communion

WHO MAY GIVE COMMUNION

The ordinary ministers of Communion are bishops, priests, and deacons. If Communion is being given under both kinds, it is especially recommended that deacons fulfill their ministry by ministering the chalice to the faithful (cf. GIRM 137).

Instituted acolytes are *de iure* (by law) extraordinary ministers of the Eucharist. Other lay persons are authorized to act as extraordinary ministers of Holy Communion. For information on acolytes and when other lay people may be used as extraordinary ministers, see chapter 2.

CANON LAW REQUIREMENTS FOR RECEIVING COMMUNION

The *Code of Canon Law* has a significant amount to say about who may receive the sacraments, including the Eucharist. The *Code's* most basic statement on the matter is this:

CANON 843 §1

The sacred ministers cannot refuse the sacraments to those who ask for them at appropriate times, are properly disposed, and are not prohibited by law from receiving them.

This canon lists three conditions that must be fulfilled for a minister to be required to give the sacraments to a person who requests them. The three conditions are (a) appropriate time, (b) proper disposition, and (c) lack of legal prohibition.

Appropriate Time

The notion of appropriate times can refer to such things as the time of day or the day of the week. For example, it would not be appropriate to ask the celebrant to hear one's confession after Mass has started. Nor would it be appropriate to ask a priest to administer the sacraments on his day off unless there were a special reason.

Regarding the Eucharist in particular, the appropriate time to receive it—though not the only time—is during Mass.

CANON 918

It is highly recommended that the faithful receive Holy Communion during the celebration of the Eucharist itself, but it should be administered outside Mass to those who request it for a just cause, the liturgical rites being observed.

When the canon speaks of the appropriate liturgical rites to be observed, it principally refers to a rite in the *Roman Ritual* titled "Holy Communion and Worship of the Eucharist Outside Mass."

This canon also sheds light on the reading of canon 843 with specific regard to receiving the Eucharist. The faithful are highly encouraged to receive the Eucharist during Mass, but Communion *should* also be administered to them outside Mass so long as there is a "just cause."

In canon law terms, a just cause is generally any reason that is not illegal. It does not even have to be a strong reason, just one that is not legally or morally forbidden. An example of a just cause would be to feed one's soul, spiritually. A just cause is among the lowest levels of justification that canon law recognizes. It is much lower, for example, than a requirement that there be a serious cause, much less a grave cause.

One situation when there is not only a just cause for receiving Communion outside of Mass but also a much stronger cause is when a sick person is in danger of death, unable to attend Mass, and unable to have Mass said where he is. The Church is very concerned that all Catholics receive the Eucharist as Viaticum in these circumstances. Viaticum is a form of Communion outside of Mass. It has a history going back to the early Church and has played a key role in preparation for death in Christian history.

The Code states:

CANON 921 §1

The Christian faithful who are in danger of death, arising from any cause, are to be nourished by Holy Communion in the form of Viaticum.

The Church is so concerned that it mandates the giving of Viaticum, if possible, before the sick person goes into a coma or becomes mentally impaired:

CANON 922

Holy Viaticum for the sick is not to be delayed too long; those who have the care of souls are to be zealous and vigilant that they are nourished by Viaticum while they are fully conscious.

If the person has become mentally impaired or fallen into a coma, however, Viaticum can still be given to the person, especially the Precious Blood under the form of wine.

Proper Dispositions

Proper disposition includes deportment, attitude, holding the Church's faith regarding the sacrament, and the state of grace (for those sacraments that do not confer the state of grace; for the sacraments that ordinarily confer the state of grace, repentance is required).

The *Catechism of the Catholic Church* sheds light on what dispositions are proper:

The Lord addresses an invitation to us, urging us to receive him in the sacrament of the Eucharist: "Truly, I say to you, unless you eat the flesh of the Son of man and drink his Blood, you have no life in you" [John 6:53].

To respond to this invitation we must prepare ourselves for so great and so holy a moment. Saint Paul urges us to examine our conscience: "Whoever, therefore, eats the bread or drinks the cup of the Lord in an unworthy manner will be guilty of profaning the Body and Blood of the Lord. Let a man examine himself, and so eat of the bread and drink of the cup. For any one who eats and drinks without discerning the Body eats and drinks judgment upon himself" [1 Cor. 11:27–29]. Anyone conscious of a grave sin must receive the sacrament of reconciliation before coming to Communion.

Before so great a sacrament, the faithful can only echo humbly and with ardent faith the words of the Centurion: "*Domine, non sum dignus ut intres sub tectum meum, sed tantum dic verbo, et sanabitur anima mea*" ("Lord, I am not worthy that you should enter under my roof, but only say the word and my soul will be healed") [Roman Missal, response to the invitation to Communion; cf. Matt. 8:8]. And in the Divine Liturgy of Saint John Chrysostom the faithful pray in the same spirit:

> *O Son of God, bring me into communion today with your mystical supper. I shall not tell your enemies the secret, nor kiss you with Judas' kiss. But like the good thief I cry, "Jesus, remember me when you come into your kingdom."*

To prepare for worthy reception of this sacrament, the faithful should observe the fast required in their Church [cf. CIC, can. 919]. Bodily demeanor (gestures, clothing) ought to convey the respect, solemnity, and joy of this moment when Christ becomes our guest [CCC 1384–1387].

Of the dispositions required to receive the Eucharist, the state of grace is *the most fundamental*. To receive the Eucharist while knowing one does not have the state of grace is to commit grave sacrilege—a mortal sin if done with adequate reflection and sufficient consent.

Because of this, the Church has legally prohibited those who have unconfessed mortal sins from receiving the Eucharist except in very specific circumstances, and even then the person must make an act of perfect contrition to try to ensure the state of grace. The Code states:

CANON 916

A person who is conscious of grave sin is not to celebrate Mass or to receive the Body of the Lord without prior sacramental confession unless a grave reason is present and there is no opportunity of confessing; in this case the person is to be mindful of the obligation to make an act of perfect contrition, including the intention of confessing as soon as possible.

A second disposition that the Church has mandated in its legislation concerns reverence for the Eucharist. One way that Christians have historically manifested their reverence for Christ's Presence in the Eucharist is by fasting before receiving it.

In the 1917 *Code of Canon Law*, the fast for the laity was to be from midnight to the time of Communion. However, in 1957, Pope Pius XII shortened it to three hours. Bishops later requested that it be shortened to one hour, and Pope Paul VI issued a concession on the Eucharistic fast that was announced at a public session of Vatican II on November 21, 1964. The announcement stated:

In view of the difficulties in many places regarding the Eucharistic fast, Pope Paul VI, acceding to the requests of the bishops, grants that the fast from solid food is shortened to one hour before Communion in the case of both priests and faithful. The concession also covers use of alcoholic beverages, but with proper moderation being observed [AAS 57 (1965) 186, DOL 2117].

Non-alcoholic drinks already had a one-hour rather than a three-hour fast (cf. DOL 2116).

The current (1983) *Code of Canon Law* frames the obligation this way:

CANON 919 §1

> One who is to receive the Most Holy Eucharist is to abstain from any food or drink, with the exception only of water and medicine, for at least the period of one hour before Holy Communion.

As this canon reveals, the Eucharistic fast currently is reckoned from the time of Communion, not the time that Mass begins. One may take food within one hour of Mass, so long as one does not take it within one hour of the time that one will receive Communion.

The prohibition also contains exceptions for drinking water and taking medicine. Canon law does not make any requirement concerning a fast from these two. Under the Code, both may be taken at any time prior to Communion. In regard to medicine, the Code makes no requirement that there be a serious reason for taking it. Aspirin to relieve a mild headache is permitted, for medicine is not considered food.

There is also no requirement that the faithful refrain from food or drink for any period *following* Communion.

In observing the Eucharistic fast, the faithful should not be overly scrupulous. The fast gains its authority from Church law. There is nothing intrinsically sinful about having other things in one's stomach at the same time as the Eucharist. Food does no injury to Jesus under the sacramental species, and it is not intrinsically disrespectful. This is clear not only from the fact that there is no requirement to fast *after* Communion, but also because the Code does not require priests to observe the fast for any Masses except the first one they celebrate during the day:

CANON 919 §2

A priest who celebrates the Most Holy Eucharist two or three times on the same day may take something before the second or third celebration even if the period of one hour does not intervene.

Because the Church's current law does not establish a canonical penalty or a specific moral gravity for violating the Eucharistic fast, it should not be considered a grave matter and should not be the subject of scrupulosity. Thus, for example, if one is not *sure* whether it has been a full hour since one last ate, this should not be an occasion of scruples to prevent one from receiving Communion. In fact, the point of reducing the Eucharistic fast was to make it easier for the faithful to receive Communion more frequently.

A final change which has occurred in the Church's law regarding the Eucharistic fast concerns those who are aged or infirm and those who care for the aged or infirm. Prior to the 1983 Code, the aged and infirm were bound to observe a fast of about a quarter of an hour and those who took care of them were only required to observe this shorter fast if it was difficult for them to observe the normal, one-hour fast. The current *Code of Canon Law* removed these obligations and simply stated:

CANON 919 §3

Those who are advanced in age or who suffer from any infirmity, as well as those who take care of them, can receive the Most Holy Eucharist even if they have taken something during the previous hour.

The Eucharistic fast is thus not binding on the aged, the infirm, or their caretakers.

Legal Prohibitions

RELIGIOUS AFFILIATION

The Code's most basic statement regarding who is legally impeded from receiving the sacraments is found in canon 844.

CANON 844 §1

Catholic ministers may licitly administer the sacraments to Catholic members of the Christian faithful only and, likewise, the latter may licitly receive the sacraments only from Catholic ministers with due regard for §§2, 3, and 4 of this canon, and canon 861 §2.

In addition to the above legal requirements for who may receive the sacraments in general, there are also specific regulations dealing with the Eucharist. The most basic of these is this:

CANON 912

Any baptized person who is not prohibited by law can and must be admitted to Holy Communion.

This is to be understood as including the conditions mentioned in 844 §1, which require the person to ask at an appropriate time and with the proper dispositions.

Under 844 §1, non-Catholics normally are legally prohibited from receiving the sacraments from a Catholic priest (canon 861 §2 explains that in an emergency situation a person other than a bishop, priest, or deacon may baptize; this does not affect the question of who may *receive* baptism) and Catholics are normally bound to receive them only from a Catholic minister. There are, however, some exceptions:

CANON 844 §2

Whenever necessity requires or genuine spiritual advantage suggests, and provided that the danger of error or indifferentism is avoided, it is lawful for the faithful for whom it is physically or morally impossible to approach a Catholic minister, to receive the sacraments of penance, Eucharist, and anointing of the sick from non-Catholic ministers in whose churches these sacraments are valid.

The churches where penance, the Eucharist, and the anointing of the sick are valid include the Eastern Orthodox churches, as well as other Eastern churches, such as the Armenian church and the Assyrian Church of the East, and also the Polish National Catholic Church, which is based in the United States. However, since the Protestant communities have not preserved valid holy orders, the three sacraments are *not valid* in standard Protestant churches, including Anglican and Episcopalian churches, and a Catholic may *not* receive these sacraments from their ministers.

Indifferentism is a heresy that states that it does not matter what Church one belongs to. The teaching of the Church is that, while those who are not formal members of the Catholic Church may be saved, one's religious affiliation is not a matter of indifference, and one does have a grave obligation to enter the Catholic Church. In fact, the *Catechism of the Catholic Church*, quoting Vatican II, states:

[T]hey could not be saved who, knowing that the Catholic Church was founded as necessary by God through Christ, would refuse either to enter it or to remain in it [CCC 846, citing Vatican II *Lumen Gentium* 14].

If one's reception of the sacraments in one of the Eastern churches or other churches where the sacraments are valid would lead oneself or others into indifferentism, then one should not receive the sacraments.

These same sacraments of the Eucharist, penance, and the anointing of the sick may also be given by Catholic priests to members of the Eastern (oriental) churches on certain conditions:

CANON 844 §3

Catholic ministers may licitly administer the sacraments of penance, Eucharist and anointing of the sick to members of the oriental churches which do not have full communion with the Catholic Church, if they ask on their own for the sacraments and are properly disposed. This holds also for members of other churches which in the judgment of the Apostolic See are in the same condition as the oriental churches as far as these sacraments are concerned.

Non-Catholics belonging to the oriental churches thus are not legally prohibited from receiving the Eucharist if they ask on their own to receive it (e.g., they have not been pressured into requesting it). This does not apply to Anglicans or Episcopalians since the Apostolic See has not judged them in the same condition as the oriental churches, due to their lack of valid holy orders. They fall under the following section of the canon, which deals with Protestants generally:

CANON 844 §4

If the danger of death is present or other grave necessity, in the judgment of the diocesan bishop or the conference of bishops, Catholic ministers may licitly administer these sacraments to other Christians who do not have full communion with the Catholic Church, who cannot approach a minister of their own community and on their own ask for it, provided they manifest Catholic faith in these sacraments and are properly disposed.

As this section of the canon makes clear, most Protestants (since they are non-Catholic Christians who do not belong to oriental churches) are only able to receive the Eucharist in very limited circumstances. Five conditions must be met: (1) there must be the danger of death or a situation which the diocesan bishop or national conference of bishops has judged to be a case of grave necessity, (2) the non-Catholic must not be able to approach a minister of his own community, (3) he must ask on his own for the sacrament, (4) he must manifest (display) Catholic faith in the sacrament (that is, believe what the Catholic Church believes concerning the sacrament), and (3) he must be properly disposed. Since conditions (1), (2), and (4) are not often met, Protestants are legally prohibited from receiving the Eucharist in most circumstances.

Marriages and funerals at which non-Catholic Christians are present often occur in America. However, these do not meet the test set out in canon 844 §4 concerning non-Catholic Christians receiving Communion. Among other things (such as the necessity of sharing the Church's beliefs regarding the Eucharist and being unable to approach a minister of their own community), the canon only permits such Communion "if the danger of death is present or other grave necessity, in the judgment of the diocesan bishop or the conference of bishops." This condition is not met on a national basis for weddings and funerals since the conference of bishops has not declared these events to create a grave necessity for non-Catholics to receive Communion. Much less has the Holy See dispensed with the other requirements of 844 §4, which would be necessary to allow Protestants in general to receive Communion at these events.

In giving penance, the Eucharist, and anointing to non-Catholics, sensitive ecumenical issues may emerge, and the heads of the local non-Catholic churches must be consulted before the diocesan bishop or national conference of bishops enacts general norms regarding the distribution of these sacraments:

CANON 844 §5

For the cases in §§2, 3, and 4, neither the diocesan bishop nor the conference of bishops is to enact general norms except after consultation with at least the local competent authority of the interested non-Catholic Church or community.

For the guidelines that the U.S. National Conference of Catholic Bishops has established, see Appendix I.

EXCOMMUNICATION, INTERDICT, AND MANIFEST GRAVE SIN

In addition to the legal prohibitions dealing with religious affiliation, the Code also includes a prohibition concerning those who have been excommunicated or interdicted:

CANON 915

Those who are excommunicated or interdicted after the imposition or declaration of the penalty and others who obstinately persist in manifest grave sin are not to be admitted to Holy Communion.

Sometimes Catholics are scandalized when priests have given Communion to public figures that have bad reputations—especially Catholic politicians who vote contrary to Catholic moral teaching or who have shaky marital records. But priests are not *allowed* to refuse a public figure Communion simply because he has a bad reputation or even because his past behavior has been scandalous. Only those who "obstinately persist in manifest grave sin" may be refused. This condition must be interpreted strictly. In establishing the norms for interpreting its canons, the Code states:

CANON 18

> Laws which establish a penalty or restrict the free exercise of rights or which contain an exception to the law are subject to a strict interpretation.

In the case of canon 915, we have a canon which restricts the free exercise of a right—the right of the baptized to the sacraments and to Communion, which is established in canons 844 §1 and 912 (cited above). Canon 915 therefore must be interpreted strictly, which means that whenever there is a doubt concerning whether a person fits the definition of one who "obstinately persists in manifest grave sin," then the question must be decided in favor of the person seeking Communion.

For a priest to deny someone Communion in this case, it must not only be true that the person sins, but that the person sins gravely, that the person's grave sins are publicly *known* (not just rumored or *assumed* to be occurring in a vague, general way, but known specifically), that he is persisting in these publicly-known sins, and that he is doing so obstinately—that he is not innocently ignorant or partially ignorant or suffering from a psychological disorder that relieves him of full accountability for his actions.

As it stands, a priest is not allowed to refuse Communion to someone just because he is a notorious individual. A much stricter test must be met, and often the public that is sitting in judgment on the situation does not have all the facts. For example, the public has no way of knowing if the notorious individual has just been to confession or what his confessor has been telling him (or not telling him) in private.

MULTIPLE RECEPTIONS OF COMMUNION

Under the 1917 *Code of Canon Law*, it was only permissible to receive Communion more than once per day in very rare circumstances (such as when one was being given Viaticum). However, under the new Code, it is permissible to receive Communion twice per day, so long as one is assisting (worshiping) at the second Mass. (This means that one could *first* receive Communion without assisting at Mass, for example, if one came into church right before Communion, but one *must* be assisting at Mass the second time in order to receive Communion.)

The current *Code of Canon Law* states:

CANON 917

A person who has received the Most Holy Eucharist may receive it again on the same day only during the celebration of the Eucharist in which the person participates, with due regard for the prescription of canon 921 §2.

The Pontifical Commission for the Authentic Interpretation of the *Code of Canon Law* clarified the interpretation by offering an authentic interpretation of it:

Dubium: Whether, according to canon 917, one who has already received the Most Holy Eucharist may receive it again on the same day only a second time, or as often as one participates in the celebration of the Eucharist?

Responsum: Affirmative to the first; negative to the second [*Canon Law Digest* (1991) 11:208].

This means that one's first Communion during the day might be (a) during a Mass which one is attending, (b) during a Mass where one is *only present* at Communion time, (c) at a public Communion service done in place of a Mass (common in areas where there is a deficiency of priests, though sometimes overused in areas), or (d) at a private Communion service where only you and the priest or extraordinary minister of

Holy Communion are present (as when Communion is sent to the sick in hospitals).

One may receive Communion a second time, but *only* during a Mass which one is attending (participating in the Mass does not mean serving as a minister at the Mass; it only requires the level of participation that ordinary worshipers in the pews have). There are a number of options for how one might receive Communion the first time during the day, but the second time *must* be in the context of a Mass one is attending.

An exception to this is found in canon 921 §2, which deals with those in danger of death:

CANON 921 §2

> Even if they have received Communion in the same day, those who are in danger of death are strongly urged to receive again.

Thus if a person in danger of death has already received Communion once, he may receive it again, even if it is not in the context of a Mass being celebrated in his presence. However, if he remains in such a critically ill situation, he should only be given Communion once per day unless he is able to make it to Mass for his second Communion of the day (not normally possible for one critically ill). The Code states:

CANON 921 §3

> While the danger of death lasts, it is recommended that Holy Communion be given repeatedly but on separate days.

FIRST COMMUNION AND CONFESSION

A special issue concerning who can go to Communion involves Latin Rite children who are receiving their First Communion. May they be admitted to Communion before they are permitted to go to the sacrament of confession? The answer, apart from exceptional circumstances, is no.

In some places in the early 1970s, parishes had been experimenting with admitting children to First Communion before permitting them to go to first confession. However, in 1973 the Sacred Congregation for the Discipline of the Sacraments strictly prohibited this experimentation. The congregation promulgated a declaration in which it reaffirmed the ruling of a 1910 decree ordered by Pope Pius X. The decree, which was written by the Sacred Congregation for the Discipline of the Sacraments, is known as *Quam Singulari,* and it prohibited the practice of not admitting children to confession prior to First Communion.

Condemning a number of related errors, *Quam Singulari* stated:

> No less worthy of condemnation is that practice which prevails in many places prohibiting from sacramental confession children who have not yet made their first Holy Communion, or of not giving them absolution. Thus it happens that they, perhaps having fallen into serious sin, remain in that very dangerous state for a long time.
>
> But worse still is the practice in certain places which prohibits children who have not yet made their First Communion from being fortified by the Holy Viaticum, even when they are in imminent danger of death . . .
>
> [D]aily approach to Communion is open to all, old and young, and two conditions only are required: the state of grace and a right intention.

The congregation then went on to explain that the age of discretion needed to receive these sacraments is the same both for confession and Communion:

The abuses which we are condemning are due to the fact that they who distinguished one age of discretion for penance and another for the Eucharist did so in error. . . .

[T]he age of discretion for confession is the time when one can distinguish between right and wrong, that is, when one arrives at a certain use of reason, and so similarly, for Holy Communion is required the age when one can distinguish between the Bread of the Holy Eucharist and ordinary bread—again the age at which a child attains the use of reason. . . .

Finally, the congregation established a number of rules regarding the admission of children to Holy Communion and confession. They included:

After careful deliberation on all these points, this Sacred Congregation of the Discipline of the Sacraments . . . has deemed it needful to prescribe the following rules which are to be observed everywhere for the First Communion of children.

1. The age of discretion, both for confession and for Holy Communion, is the time when a child begins to reason, that is about the seventh year, more or less. From that time on begins the obligation of fulfilling the precept of both confession and Communion.

2. A full and perfect knowledge of Christian doctrine is not necessary either for first confession or for First Communion. Afterwards, however, the child will be obliged to learn gradually the entire Catechism according to his ability.

7. The custom of not admitting children to confession or of not giving them absolution when they have already attained the use of reason must be entirely abandoned. The Ordinary shall see to it that this condition ceases absolutely, and he may, if necessary, use legal measures accordingly.

8. The practice of not administering Viaticum and Extreme Unction to children who have attained the use of reason, and of burying them with the rite used for infants is a most intolerable

abuse. The Ordinary should take very severe measures against those who do not give up the practice.

Basing itself on this, in 1973 the Congregation for the Discipline of the Sacraments stated:

> [N]ew practices [recently have been] introduced in some regions whereby reception of the Eucharist was permitted before reception of the sacrament of penance . . . .
>
> The Congregations for the Discipline of the Sacraments and for the Clergy have considered this matter thoroughly and taken into account the views of the conferences of bishops. With the approval of Pope Paul VI, therefore, the two Congregations by the present document declare that an end must be put to these experiments—which have now gone on for three years . . . and that thereafter the Decree *Quam Singulari* must be obeyed everywhere by all [*Sanctus Pontifex*, 24 May 1973; AAS 65 (1973) 410, DOL 3141–3142].

The Holy See has *repeatedly* reiterated this prohibition on admitting children to the Eucharist without permitting them to go to confession. The current *Code of Canon Law* states:

> CANON 914
>
> It is the responsibility, in the first place, of parents and those who take the place of parents as well as of the pastor to see that children who have reached the use of reason are correctly prepared and are nourished by the divine food as early as possible, preceded by sacramental confession; it is also for the pastor to be vigilant lest any children come to the Holy Banquet who have not reached the use of reason or whom he judges are not sufficiently disposed.

The age of reason, also determined by the Code, is established for canonical purposes as generally being seven years of age (CIC 11). One cannot state that children in general past this age do not have sufficient reason for admission to the sacraments; one can only say that certain *individual* children have an intellectual or emotional problem that deprives them of the reason that normal children have at this age.

Though it is not a work of canon law, the *Catechism of the Catholic Church* is even more forceful concerning the need for children to go to confession prior to First Communion. It states:

> Children must go to the sacrament of penance before receiving Communion for the first time [CCC 1457].

Parents who wish their children to go to first confession prior to First Communion are sometimes told that the children must be properly catechized for confession before they may be admitted. This is not true. While the *Code of Canon Law* does require prior catechesis for "the sacraments of the living" —baptism, confirmation, the Holy Eucharist, orders, and marriage—it does not require prior catechesis for "the sacraments of the dead"—confession and anointing, which minister to those who are spiritually dead or in danger of physical death.

Canonist Dr. Edward Peters discusses this in the following question:

> *Q: Our son is preparing for First Communion. When we spoke with the DRE in our parish about his also receiving the sacrament of penance, we were told that he cannot make his confession because our parish does not offer catechesis for confession until two years after First Communion. This does not seem right to us.*

> A: Telling a child (or the parents of a child inquiring on his behalf) that he cannot receive the sacrament of penance because "the parish does not offer catechesis for confession" until some future time is faulty in several respects. Let me outline just one serious problem with what you've been told.

Strictly speaking, the 1983 *Code of Canon Law* does not require any catechesis prior to reception of the sacrament of penance. Unlike baptism (canon 865), confirmation (canon 889), Eucharist (canon 913), holy orders (canon 1028), or matrimony (canon 1063), all of which explicitly require various degrees of instruction prior to reception of the sacrament, the only thing required for reception of confession is contrition for sins (canon 987). No conscientious parent rejects a young child's attempt to say "sorry" for something just because that child has not yet been formally instructed in the notion of contrition and forgiveness, and the Church does not prevent her children from expressing sorrow for sins just because of a lack of prior instruction in the area. By the same token, and with the same reasoning, the other sacrament of healing, anointing of the sick, requires nothing by way of prior catechesis for licit reception (canon 1004).

Don't misunderstand me: I think catechesis for confession is a fine thing and it should be offered. It can deepen one's sense of personal sorrow for sin, heighten one's awareness of the obligation to avoid sin in the future, open one's eyes to the abundant mercy of God, and generally facilitate a fruitful reception of the sacrament. But to prevent a child from approaching the sacrament of penance simply because "we haven't taught him how to do it yet" is, at best, an unconvincing excuse for withholding a sacrament and, at worst, a violation of the child's fundamental right, as a member of the faithful, to approach his ministers for the sacraments in general (canon 213) and to access the graces of confession in particular (canon 991) [*This Rock* 8:10:41 (October 1997)].

There is no canonical requirement for any formal catechesis on confession. Some catechesis, at least informally, is useful. However, this does not have to take place in a formal, classroom setting. The parents themselves may give this instruction.

It is the duty of the priest to make sure the child is properly disposed for confession, but what counts as proper disposition for the sacrament of penance is specified in the Code, and it does *not* include prior catechesis:

CANON 987

In order to receive the salvific remedy of the sacrament of penance, the Christian faithful ought to be so disposed that, having repudiated the sins committed and having a purpose of amendment, they are converted to God.

To go to the sacrament of penance, one only needs to convert to God by repudiating of the sins against God and having purpose of amendment. One does not need extensive catechesis in the different kinds or gravities of sins.

The Code is also specific about the duty of pastors not only to ensure the faithful in their care have access to the sacraments in general but also to guarantee their access to confession in particular:

CANON 986 §1

All to whom the care of souls is committed by reason of an office are obliged to provide that the confession of the faithful entrusted to their care can be heard when they reasonably ask to be heard and that the opportunity be given to them to come to individual confession on days and hours set for their convenience.

This is important because once a person has attained the age of discretion one has a positive *obligation* to confess one's grave sins annually.

CANON 989

After having attained the age of discretion, each of the faithful is bound by an obligation faithfully to confess serious [Latin, *gravia*, or "grave"] sins at least once a year.

For a pastor to deny a child of his parish the opportunity to confess his grave sins annually after that child has reached the age of discretion (cf. CIC 11) is to prevent the child from doing something he has an obligation to do.

One case in which children would not be going to confession prior to Communion would be when parents who belong to the Latin church have their child baptized in an Eastern Rite Catholic parish (not the same as an Eastern Orthodox church). In many Eastern Rites, infants receive baptism, confirmation (referred to in the Eastern Rites as *chrismation*), and First Communion at the same time. Some parents belonging to Latin Rite churches have chosen to have their infant baptized and confirmed and admitted to the Eucharist in an Eastern Rite Catholic parish. The Eastern Rite equivalent to the *Code of Canon Law*, a work known as the *Code of Canons of the Eastern Churches* (CCEO), states:

CANON 696

§1. All presbyters [priests] of the Eastern Churches can validly administer this sacrament [chrismation, or confirmation] either along with baptism or separately to all the Christian faithful of any Church *sui iuris* [church with its own law], including the Latin church.

§2. The Christian faithful of the Eastern Churches validly receive this sacrament also from presbyters of the Latin Church, according to the faculties with which these are endowed.

§3. Any presbyter licitly administers this sacrament only to the Christian faithful of his own Church *sui iuris*; when it is a case of Christian faithful of other Churches *sui iuris*, he lawfully acts if they are his subjects, or those whom he lawfully baptizes in virtue of another title, or those who are in danger of death, and always with due regard for the agreements entered between the Churches *sui iuris* in this matter.

In the Latin church's *Code of Canon Law*, the term "subject" typically refers to one in the geographical region of a parish or church, whereas Eastern canon law operates predominantly personally rather than territorially.

A child baptized, confirmed, and admitted to the Eucharist in an Eastern Rite Catholic church remains a member of the Latin church if he has Latin Rite parents, since that would be the ecclesiastical title to which he was ascribed at his baptism. Unless special circumstances prevail, a child is always ascribed to the ritual church to which his parents belong (cf. canon 111 for rules governing when a child is a member of the Latin church). Merely receiving baptism in an Eastern Rite Catholic church "does not carry with it enrollment in that church" (CIC 112 §2).

Manner of Receiving Communion

Because Christ himself is under the sacred species, great reverence must be shown to them, and the Church has laid out specific rules concerning how Communion is to be received. For example, individuals may not administer Communion to themselves, a practice known as self-communication.

SELF-COMMUNICATION NOT PERMITTED

Communicants may not pick up the sacred Host from the ciborium or the sacred chalice from an altar or table. *Inaestimabile Donum* states:

> Communion is a gift of the Lord, given to the faithful through the minister appointed for this purpose. It is not permitted that the faithful should themselves pick up the consecrated bread and the sacred chalice, still less that they should hand them from one to another [ID 9].

The same concern that individuals do not self-communicate is expressed in the U.S. bishops' directory, *This Holy and Living Sacrifice: Directory for the Celebration and Reception of Communion under Both Kinds,* which was approved by the Holy See in 1984. It states:

> The chalice may never be left on the altar or another place to be picked up by the communicant for self-communication (except in the case of concelebrating bishops or priests), nor may the chalice be passed from one communicant to another. There shall always be a minister of the cup [HLS 46].

Though they may not pick up the chalice, communicants do take the chalice from the priest or extraordinary minister of Holy Communion when receiving Communion under both kinds. It is *not* a liturgical abuse for the priest or extraordinary minister to hand the chalice to the communicant.

A special case of self-communication involves Communion by intinction. Even though the communicant may have been handed the Host by the priest, the communicant may not dip it into the chalice, but must give it to the deacon or other minister to be dipped in the Precious Blood on his behalf. Following this, he must receive on the tongue rather than in the hand:

> Reception of the Precious Blood . . . by intinction may remove the communicant's legitimate option to receive Communion in the hand or, for valid reasons, not to receive the consecrated wine. However, if Communion is given by intinction the communicant may never dip the Eucharistic bread into the chalice. Communion under either the form of bread or wine must always be given by a minister with the usual words [*ibid.*, 52].

Manner of Receiving the Host

The rubrics of the Mass state that at Communion time the priest (or other minister) takes the paten or other vessel and goes to the communicants. He takes a host for each one, raises it a little, and shows it, saying: *The Body of Christ*. The communicant answers: *Amen* and receives Communion.

Although Communion on the tongue was the exclusive practice of the Latin Rite of the Church until recently, Communion in the hand was practiced in the early Church. For example, Saint Cyril of Jerusalem instructed his newly baptized Christians:

> In approaching [Communion], therefore, come not with thy wrists extended or thy fingers spread; but make thy left hand a throne for the right, as for that which is to receive a King. And having hollowed thy palm, receive the Body of Christ, saying over it, *Amen*. So then after having carefully hallowed thine eyes by the touch of the Holy Body, partake of it; giving heed lest thou lose any portion thereof; for whatever thou losest, is evidently a loss to thee as it were from one of thine own members [*Catechetical Lectures* 23:21].

Today, communicants in dioceses within the U.S. may choose to receive the Host in the hand or on the tongue (except in cases of intinction—dipping the Host into the chalice—in which case one must always receive the dipped Host on the tongue; see below):

> On June 17, 1977, the Congregation of Sacraments and Divine Worship approved the request of the National Conference of Catholic Bishops to permit the optional practice of Communion in the hand. The Bishops' Committee on the Liturgy, in its catechesis about this optional practice, drew attention to these considerations:
>
> a. Proper catechesis must be provided to assure the proper and reverent reception of Communion without any suggestion of wavering on the part of the Church in its faith in the Eucharistic presence.

b. The practice must remain the option of the communicant. The priest or minister of Communion does not make the decision as to the manner of reception of Communion. It is the communicant's personal choice.

c. When Communion is distributed under both kinds by intinction, the Host is not placed in the hands of the communicants, nor may the communicants receive the Host and dip it into the chalice. Intinction should not be introduced as a means of circumventing the practice of Communion in the hand.

d. Children have the option to receive Communion in the hand or on the tongue. No limitations because of age have been established. Careful preparation for the first reception of the Eucharist will provide the necessary instruction [AGI 240].

From some areas, there are reports of priests insisting that people receive Communion in the hand. This is a liturgical abuse, for the American *Appendix to the General Instruction*, as found in the Sacramentary, states that the practice of receiving in the hand "*must remain the option of the communicant. The priest or minister of Communion does not make the decision*," the only exception being Communion by intinction, when one must receive Communion on the tongue.

This choice applies even to extraordinary ministers of Holy Communion. Some priests are reported to have insisted that extraordinary ministers receive in the hand. This is not permitted. No exception is made for treating extraordinary ministers different than other communicants in this regard. A priest certainly could *ask* extraordinary ministers to receive in the hand, but he may not *insist* or *require* that they do so.

In fact, GIRM presupposes that extraordinary ministers, like other communicants, will be receiving on the tongue apart from the special permission which has now been granted to receive in the hand (see GIRM 117, quoted in the section on the sequence of receiving Communion, below).

COMMUNION FROM THE CHALICE

In the early Church, it was also common for the faithful to receive the Eucharist under the form of wine as well as under the form of bread. For example, Saint Cyril of Jerusalem states:

> Then, after thou hast partaken of the Body of Christ, draw near also to the cup of his Blood; not stretching forth thine hands, but bending, and saying with an air of worship and reverence, *Amen*, hallow thyself by partaking also of the Blood of Christ [*Catechetical Lectures* 23:22].

However, there were also many cases in the early Church where Communion was received only under the form of bread. In part, this was because it was often hard to hold celebrations of the liturgy and receiving Communion under the form of bread allowed Christians to reserve the Host in their houses and receive daily Communion even when celebrations of the liturgy were not possible on a daily basis. Communion under one kind became the normal practice in many places by the late Middle Ages. When the Protestant Reformers began to leave the Church, they often protested against the reception of Communion only under one kind, just as they protested against the use of Latin as a liturgical language.

In response, the Council of Trent protected the historic Christian teaching that Communion under one kind was valid by maintaining the standard practice whereby most people received Communion under one kind.

By the twentieth century, things had changed, and there was no movement within the Catholic Church denying the validity of Communion under only one kind. Thus the Second Vatican Council reviewed the situation and allowed for a greater use of Communion under both kinds. The *General Instruction of the Roman Missal* states:

Moved by [a] spirit and pastoral concern, Vatican II was able to reevaluate the Tridentine norm on Communion under both kinds. No one today challenges the doctrinal principles on the completeness of Eucharistic Communion under the form of bread alone. The Council thus gave permission for the reception of Communion under both kinds on some occasions, because this more explicit form of the sacramental sign offers a special means of deepening the understanding of the mystery in which the faithful are taking part [GIRM Introduction, 14].

The discipline of Communion under both kinds has been largely restored in many parts of the Latin Rite today. There has been no change in doctrine, however. The *General Instruction* states:

> For the faithful who take part in the rite or are present at it, pastors should take care to call to mind as clearly as possible the Catholic teaching according to the Council of Trent on the manner of Communion. Above all they should instruct the people that according to the Catholic faith Christ, whole and entire, as well as the true sacrament are received even under one kind only; that, therefore, as far as the effects are concerned, those who receive in this manner are not deprived of any necessary grace for salvation.
>
> Pastors are also to teach that the Church has power in its stewardship of the sacraments, provided their substance remains intact. The Church may make those rules and changes that, in view of the different conditions, times, and places, it decides to be in the interest of reverence for the sacraments or the well-being of the recipients. At the same time the faithful should be guided toward a desire to take part more intensely in a sacred rite in which the sign of the Eucharistic meal stands out more explicitly [GIRM 241].

In the United States, it is frequently permissible to receive Communion under both kinds (that is, both the Host and from the chalice). In the U.S. bishops' *Appendix to the General Instruction for the Dioceses of the United States*, it is noted that in November, 1970, the bishops approved the giving of Communion under both kinds at weekday Masses (AGI 242:19).

This permission was further extended in the publication of the U.S. bishops' directory, *This Holy and Living Sacrifice: Directory for the Celebration and Reception of Communion under Both Kinds,* which was approved by the Holy See in 1984. This document stated that, in addition to weekday Masses,

> Communion under both kinds is also permitted at parish and community Masses celebrated on Sundays and holy days of obligation in the dioceses of the United States [HLS 21].

The only Masses at which Communion under both kinds is not currently permitted in the U.S. are ones with a great number of communicants that would prevent the orderly and reverent reception of Communion under both kinds or other circumstances where the orderly and reverent reception of the Precious Blood is doubtful (these situations are described in HLS 22; see p. 248).

The Precious Blood can be administered in a number of ways. However, the preferred way is for the communicant to drink from the chalice:

> Because of its ancient sign value "*ex institutione Christi*" [of Christ's institution], Communion from the cup or chalice is always to be preferred to any other form of ministering the Precious Blood [HLS 44].

The principal alternative to drinking from the cup is communication by intinction, in which case the minister dips the consecrated Host into the Precious Blood and then places it on the tongue of the communicant.

> Communion may also be given by intinction. However, care is to be taken that the Eucharistic bread is not too thin or too

small, but a little thicker than usual so that after being partly dipped into the Precious Blood, it can still easily be given to the communicant.

[This form] of receiving the Precious Blood . . . [is] not customary in the United States [*ibid., 50c–51*].

Different words are used to administer Communion depending on the manner in which it is given:

The chalice is always offered to the communicant with the words "The Blood of Christ," to which the communicant responds, "Amen."

When Communion is given by intinction, the minister shall say, "The Body and Blood of Christ," to which the communicant responds, "Amen." [HLS 45].

When the communicants drink from the cup there is a brief purification performed after each one has received the Precious Blood:

After each communicant has received the Blood of Christ, the minister shall carefully wipe both sides of the rim of the cup with a purificator. This action is both a matter of courtesy and hygiene. It is also customary for the minister to move the chalice a quarter turn after each communicant for the same reasons [HLS 47].

In no case may the faithful be *required* to receive the Precious Blood when Communion is offered from the chalice:

When Communion from the cup is offered to the assembly, it shall always be clear that it is the option of the communicant and not of the minister whether the communicant shall receive the consecrated wine. Of course, pastors should encourage the whole assembly to receive Communion under both kinds [HLS 48].

For a valid reason, however, a person who chooses to receive Communion may be required to receive it by intinction if that is the form in which it is being administered (see quotation from HLS 52 in the section on self-communication, above).

Children are allowed to receive the Precious Blood when it is offered to the faithful. However, particular attention needs to be paid to make sure they receive it properly and reverently:

> Special care shall be given when children receive Communion from the chalice. Parents should be instructed that Communion under both kinds is an ancient tradition for children old enough to drink from a cup. However, children should have some familiarity with drinking wine at home before they are offered the chalice [HLS 49].

With regard to posture during Communion—whether one can receive kneeling or standing—please see the section on posture at Mass in chapter 11.

Sequence of the Communion Rite

LORD'S PRAYER OR "OUR FATHER"

The Communion rite begins with the recitation of the Our Father. The *General Instruction* describes the significance of this prayer for the liturgy as follows:

> Lord's Prayer: this is a petition both for daily food, which for Christians means also the Eucharistic Bread, and for the forgiveness of sin, so that what is holy may be given to those who are holy. The priest offers the invitation to pray, but all the faithful say the prayer with him; he alone adds the embolism, *Deliver us*, which the people conclude with a doxology. The embolism, developing the last petition of the Lord's Prayer, begs on behalf of the entire community of the faithful deliverance from the power of evil. The invitation, the prayer itself, the embolism,

and the people's doxology are sung or are recited aloud [GIRM 5a].

The final doxology said by the people "For thine is the kingdom and the power and the glory, for ever and ever. Amen" is an ancient one. It appears in some ancient manuscripts as part of Matthew 6:13, though it was probably not in the original of Matthew's Gospel but was added by a scribe because of its use in the liturgy. Though absent from the liturgy for some time, it has recently been restored.

Concerning this final doxology, the *Catechism of the Catholic Church* states:

> The final doxology, "For the kingdom, the power and the glory are yours, now and forever," takes up again, by inclusion, the first three petitions to our Father: the glorification of his name, the coming of his reign, and the power of his saving will. But these prayers are now proclaimed as adoration and thanksgiving, as in the liturgy of heaven (cf. Rev. 1:6; 4:11; 5:13). The ruler of this world has mendaciously attributed to himself the three titles of kingship, power, and glory (cf. Luke 4:5–6). Christ, the Lord, restores them to his Father and our Father, until he hands over the kingdom to him when the mystery of salvation will be brought to its completion and God will be all in all (1 Cor. 15:24–28) [CCC 2855].

One of the most commonly asked questions concerns the holding of hands during the Our Father. The Holy See has not ruled directly on this issue. In a response to a query, however, the Holy See stated that holding hands "is a liturgical gesture introduced spontaneously but on personal initiative; it is not in the rubrics" (*Notitiae* 11 [1975] 226, DOL 1502 n. R29). For this reason, no one can be required to hold hands during the Our Father.

People also ask whether the embolism, *Deliver us*, may be omitted, especially when the concluding doxology is sung. The answer is no. Priests are directed to say the embolism even in Masses without a congregation (GIRM 224). When the Lord's Prayer and its doxology are sung, the priest alone sings the embolism between the two. In 1972 the Sacred Congregation for Divine Worship issued an instruction which directed:

After . . . the Eucharistic Prayer, all sing the acclamation, *Amen*. Then the priest alone pronounces the invitation for the Lord's Prayer and all sing it with him. The priest alone continues [singing] with the embolism, and all join in the concluding doxology [*Ordo Cantus Missae* 15; DOL 4294].

Rite of Peace

Following the recitation of the Our Father is the rite of peace. The *General Instruction* explains its purpose:

Rite of Peace: Before they share in the same bread, the faithful implore peace and unity for the Church and for the whole human family and offer some sign of their love for one another.

The form the sign of peace should take is left to the conference of bishops to determine, in accord with the culture and customs of the people [GIRM 56b].

Regarding the use of the sign of peace, the *General Instruction* states:

Then the priest says aloud the prayer, *Lord Jesus Christ*. After this prayer, extending then joining his hands, he gives the greeting of peace: *The peace of the Lord be with you always*. The people answer: *And also with you*. Then the priest may add: *Let us offer each other a sign of peace*. All exchange some sign of peace and love, according to local custom. The priest may give the sign of peace to the ministers [GIRM 112].

Since the text states that "Then the priest *may add* . . ." and not "Then the priest *says* . . ." the individual exchange of a sign of peace is optional. It is not a liturgical abuse for a priest either to call for or to omit the invitation for the people to exchange signs of peace among themselves. However, the priest is not authorized to relocate the individual exchange of a sign of peace to another part of the Mass. The U. S. Bishops have proposed relocating it to the beginning of the liturgy of the Eucharist, but the Holy See has not yet approved this.

Common sense also indicates that the individual exchange of a sign of peace should be concluded before the fraction rite begins, since the attention of the faithful should be directed to the fraction rite once it is started, not to a continuing individual exchange of signs of peace.

If the priest does call for the individual exchange of a sign of peace, he has the option of himself remaining still or of personally exchanging a sign of peace with the ministers. He is not authorized to leave the sanctuary and shake hands or hug people in the congregation, as this would unduly prolong the sign of peace and disturb the orderly flow of the liturgy.

Regarding the form that the sign of peace is to take, the U.S. bishops have said this:

> The Conference of Bishops has left the development of special modes of exchanging the sign of peace to local usage. Neither a specific form nor specific words are determined (November 1969). See the statement of the Bishops' Committee on the Liturgy, *The Sign of Peace* (1977) [AGI 56b].

If a deacon is present then he, rather than the priest, may call for the people to exchange signs of peace among themselves. The rubrics state:

> After the priest has said the prayer for peace and the greeting: *The peace of the Lord be with you always,* and the people have

made the response: *And also with you,* the deacon may invite all to exchange the sign of peace, saying *Let us offer each other the sign of peace.* He himself receives the sign of peace from the priest and may offer it to the ministers near him [GIRM 136].

There is no set formula of words that is to be used if the faithful exchange the sign of peace among each other. In many places, it is customary to say, "The peace of Christ be with you," but a particular formula is not found in the rubrics of Mass. In fact, the *Ceremonial of Bishops* states:

> The exchange of the sign of peace may be accompanied by the words, *Peace be with you,* and in the response, *And also with you.* But other words may be used in accordance with the local custom [CB 103].

Since the U.S. bishops have left the formula open, a person is free to use whatever words he wishes when individually exchanging a sign of peace.

FRACTION RITE, COMMINGLING, AND *AGNUS DEI*

The fraction rite, or "breaking of the Bread" follows the rite of peace. "Breaking of the Bread" is an ancient term for the Eucharistic liturgy. It goes back to apostolic days, following Christ's breaking of the Bread at the Last Supper (Acts 2:42, 46; cf. Luke 22:19). This use of the term "Bread" follows Christ's own description of himself as "the Bread of Life" (John 6:48) and Saint Paul's references to the Eucharist *according to appearances,* such as "The bread which we break, is it not a participation in the Body of Christ?" (1 Cor. 10:16).

At the time when the priest's Host is broken, he also drops a small part of it into the chalice. This is called the *commingling.* This originally developed from a practice known as the *fermentum*, whereby a fragment from one Host was broken off and sent to another celebration of the Eucharist, to reveal the continuity of the Church in the Eucharistic sacrifice. This custom fell out of use over time and other interpretations of the significance of the commingling have been offered, such as that it signifies the reunification of Christ's Body and Blood in his glorious, resurrected Body.

While the fraction rite and commingling are taking place, the prayer *Agnus Dei* or "Lamb of God" is sung or recited.

The *General Instruction* offers the following description of this part of the Mass:

> Breaking of the bread: In apostolic times this gesture of Christ at the Last Supper gave the entire Eucharistic action its name. This rite is not simply functional, but is a sign that in sharing in the one bread of life which is Christ, we who are many are made one Body (see 1 Cor. 10:17).
>
> Commingling: The celebrant drops a part of the Host into the chalice.
>
> *Agnus Dei:* During the breaking of the bread and the commingling, the *Agnus Dei* is as a rule sung by the choir or cantor with the congregation responding; otherwise it is recited aloud. This invocation may be repeated as often as necessary to accompany the breaking of the bread. The final reprise concludes with the words, *grant us peace* [GIRM 56c–e].

Personal Preparation for Communion

Both the priest and the people now make a personal act of preparation to receive Communion:

> Personal preparation of the priest: the priest prepares himself by the prayer, said softly, that he may receive Christ's Body and Blood to good effect. The faithful do the same by silent prayer [GIRM 56f].

The priest then shows the Host to the people. The rubrics of the Sacramentary specify:

> The priest genuflects. Taking the Host, he raises it slightly over the paten and, facing the people, says aloud:
>
> > *This is the Lamb of God who takes away the sins of the world. Happy are those who are called to his supper.*
>
> He adds, once only, with the people:
>
> > *Lord, I am not worthy to receive you, but only say the word and I shall be healed.*

RECEPTION OF COMMUNION

The priest then takes Communion. The rubrics specify the manner in which he is to do this:

> Facing the altar, the priest says inaudibly:
>
> > *May the Body of Christ bring me to everlasting life.*
>
> He reverently consumes the Body of Christ. Then he takes the chalice and says inaudibly:
>
> > *May the Blood of Christ bring me to everlasting life.*
>
> He reverently drinks the Blood of Christ.

The rubrics specify what the priest is to say as his private prayer and that he is to say it inaudibly. It is not a problem if he can be very faintly heard (if he is wearing a sensitive microphone, it may be very difficult for him *not* to be heard), especially if he is only heard by a few, but he should not deliberately speak loudly enough to be heard by all, nor should he change the words of the prayer—e.g., "May the Body/Blood of Christ bring *us* to everlasting life."

It is also important that he receive Communion first, before the faithful do, as the following rubrics indicate:

After this [i.e., after his own Communion] he takes the paten or other vessel and goes to the communicants. He takes a Host for each one, raises it a little, and shows it, saying:

The Body of Christ.

The communicant answers:

Amen.

And receives Communion.

When a deacon gives Communion, he does the same.

It is clear from a variety of sources that the priest is to receive Communion prior to the faithful (e.g., GIRM 116–117). It is also clear that the deacon is to receive Communion after the priest and before the people:

After the priest's Communion, the deacon receives under both kinds then assists the priest in giving Communion to the people. But if the Communion is under both kinds, the deacon ministers the chalice to the communicants and is the last to drink from it [GIRM 137].

It is, therefore, not permitted for the deacon and the priest to receive Communion at the same time.

Furthermore, it is even less appropriate and, therefore, not permitted for extraordinary ministers of Holy Communion to receive at the same time as the priest. If even a deacon—a person who has the sacrament of holy orders and who counts as an *ordinary* minister of Communion—does not receive Communion at the same time as the priest, then *extraordinary* ministers certainly should not. It is, in fact, an immemorial custom for assisting bishops, presbyters, deacons, acolytes, and other ministers to receive Communion after the principal celebrant.

This has the force of law, as indicated in the recent instruction on collaboration:

To avoid creating confusion, certain practices are to be avoided and eliminated where such have emerged in particular Churches [including] extraordinary ministers receiving Holy Communion apart from the other faithful as though concelebrants [ICP, Practical Provisions 8 §2].

The strong statement—that the practice must be *eliminated* of having extraordinary ministers receive Communion at the same time as the priest, apart from the rest of the faithful— shows how serious the Holy See is on this matter. The priest must receive Communion first, then the extraordinary ministers, and then the faithful.

During the course of Communion, it is also typical that a Communion song be sung:

During the priest's and the faithful's reception of the sacrament, the Communion song is sung. Its function is to express outwardly the communicants' union in spirit by means of the unity of their voices, to give evidence of joy of heart, and to make the procession to receive Christ's Body more fully an act of community. The song begins when the priest takes Communion and continues for as long as seems appropriate while the faithful receive Christ's Body. But the Communion song should be ended in good time whenever there is to be a hymn after Communion.

An antiphon from the *Graduale Romanum* may also be used with or without the psalm, or an antiphon with psalm from the Simple Gradual or another suitable song approved by the conference of bishops. It is sung by the choir alone or by the choir or cantor with the congregation.

If there is no singing, the Communion antiphon in the Missal is recited either by the people, by some of them, or by a reader. Otherwise the priest himself says it after he has received Communion and before he gives Communion to the faithful [GIRM 56i].

SILENCE AFTER COMMUNION

In many parishes, after Communion has been administered, it is customary to pause for a few moments in silent prayer. This is indeed an option, but it is not the only one:

> After Communion, the priest and people may spend some time in silent prayer. If desired, a hymn, psalm, or other song of praise may be sung by the entire congregation [GIRM 56j].
>
> Afterward [i.e., after Communion] the priest may return to the chair. A period of silence may now be observed, or a hymn of praise or a psalm may be sung [GIRM 121].

Note that the priest *may* return to the chair. He does not have to do so. Also, in many places there is a custom where people kneel following Communion until the priest sits down or until the Holy Eucharist has been reserved in the Tabernacle. Both of these are fine customs. It is important to know, however, that they are not mandated in the rubrics.

As chapter 11 shows, there is no mandated posture following Communion. Individuals may stand, sit, or kneel at their preference; they may do whatever they feel best promotes their own personal devotion to Christ in the Eucharist. As a result, people do not need to be scrupulous about when they or others begin sitting after Communion and do not need to relate it to the actions of the priest or other ministers.

If there is not a pause for silent prayer at this time, it remains incumbent on the faithful to express their gratitude and devotion by making an act of thanksgiving after they have received our Lord in Holy Communion. In many places, however, people fail to do this. Some people even leave the church building as soon as they receive Communion. As a result, the Holy See has stated that

The faithful are to be recommended not to omit to make a proper thanksgiving after Communion. They may do this during the celebration with a period of silence, with a hymn, psalm or other song of praise, or also after the celebration, if possible by staying behind to pray for a suitable time [ID 17].

PURIFICATION OF VESSELS

During the silence or song the vessels may be cleansed. However, they may also be cleansed after Mass has ended:

After Communion the priest returns to the altar and collects any remaining particles. Then, standing at the side of the altar or at a side table, he purifies the paten or ciborium over the chalice, then he purifies the chalice, saying inaudibly: *Lord, may I receive these gifts, etc.,* and dries it with a purificator. If this is done at the altar, the vessels are taken to a side table by a minister. It is also permitted, especially if there are several vessels to be purified, to leave them, properly covered and on a corporal, either at the altar or at a side table and to purify them after Mass when the people have left [GIRM 120].

Great care must be given to particles of the consecrated elements. The *General Instruction* states:

Whenever a particle of the Eucharistic bread adheres to his fingers, especially after the breaking of the bread or the Communion of the people, the priest cleanses his fingers over the paten or, if necessary, washes them. He also gathers any particles that may fall outside the paten.

The vessels are purified by the priest or else by the deacon or acolyte after the Communion or after Mass, if possible at the side table. Wine and water or water alone are used for the purification of the chalice, then drunk by the one who purifies it. The paten is usually wiped with the purificator.

If any Eucharistic bread or any particle of it should fall, it is to be picked up reverently. If any of the Precious Blood spills, the

areas should be washed and the water poured into the sacrarium
[GIRM 237–239].

The purificator is the piece of white linen used by the priest
during Mass. A sacrarium is a special sink in the sacristy that
leads down into the earth rather than into the sewer system.
Sacraria have been in use in Catholic churches for a very long
time. They are used to dispose of *water* that has been used to
purify the liturgical vessels and linens, but the sacred species
themselves may *not* be put into a sacrarium. The sacred species
must be consumed or reserved or, in exceptional instances,
dissolved so that the Real Presence no longer remains and the
resulting *water* disposed of through the sacrarium.

Dissolving the sacred species of wine, for example, is indicated in GIRM 239 (above) when the Precious Blood has been
spilled. One would dissolve a particle of a Host, for example,
if it had become so soiled (such as by regurgitation) that it is
inedible. In both cases, by dissolving the sacred species, the
appearances of bread and wine, and thus the Real Presence,
no longer remain and only water is left. Only this water, not
species concealing the Real Presence, may be put into a sacrarium.

The Holy See also clarified what is to be done with particles
of the Eucharist that are recovered:

> *Query: The GIRM no. 237 says that particles of the Eucharistic bread
> are to be collected after the consecration, but it is not clear what is to be
> done about them.*

> Reply: The GIRM no. 237 must be taken in context with other
> articles that deal with the same point. The description of the
> basic form of celebration says clearly: "After Communion the
> priest returns to the altar and collects any remaining particles.
> Then, standing at the side of the altar or at the side table, he
> purifies the paten or ciborium *over the chalice*, then purifies the

chalice . . . and dries it with a purificator" (GIRM no. 120). The Order of Mass with a congregation no. 138 says: "After Communion the priest or deacon purifies the paten *over the chalice* and the chalice itself." The Order of Mass without a congregation no. 31 says: "Then the priest purifies the chalice *over the paten* and the chalice itself." The point, therefore, is quite clear [*Notitiae* 8 (1972) 195, DOL 1627 n. R41].

It also clarified who purifies the vessels and where the purification is to be done.

Query: *After the distribution of Communion the priest often is observed purifying the vessels (chalice, paten, ciborium) at the middle of the altar. Cannot a better place and time be chosen to do this? May another minister purify the vessels?*

Reply: a. The directives in the GIRM are to be observed. There is a general principle in no. 238: "The vessels are purified by the priest or else by the deacon or acolyte after the Communion or after Mass, if possible at a side table." The directive as to time (whether after Communion or after Mass) is completed in no. 229 with one regarding place (at the side of the altar). It is implicit in this regulation that the celebrant never stands at the middle of the altar as he purifies the vessels (see also no. 120) [*Notitiae* 14 (1978) 593–594, no. 15, DOL 1628 n. R42].

The section of the *General Instruction* cited but not quoted above reads:

The chalice is washed at the side of the altar and then may be carried by the server to a side table or left on the altar, as at the beginning [GIRM 229].

In the *General Instruction* this is found in the context of regulations governing a Mass without a congregation, however, the above reply in *Notitiae* makes it clear that it also applies to Masses with a congregation, so that "the celebrant never stands at the middle of the altar as he purifies the vessels."

RESERVATION OF THE EUCHARIST

After Communion, any of the consecrated elements that remain must be consumed or reserved. *Inaestimabile Donum* explains:

> Even after Communion the Lord remains present under the species. Accordingly, when Communion has been distributed, the sacred particles remaining are to be consumed or taken by the competent minister to the place where the Eucharist is reserved.
>
> On the other hand, the consecrated wine is to be consumed immediately after Communion and may not be kept. Care must be taken to consecrate only the amount of wine needed for Communion.
>
> The rules laid down for the purification of the chalice and the other sacred vessels that have contained the Eucharistic species must be observed [ID 13–15].

This Holy and Living Sacrifice, a document approved by the Holy See in 1984 for use in the United States, instructs that:

> Ministers shall always show the greatest reverence for the Eucharistic species by their demeanor and in the manner in which they handle the consecrated bread or wine. . . .
>
> After Communion the Eucharistic bread that remains is to be stored in the tabernacle. Care should be taken in regard to any fragments remaining on the corporal or in the sacred vessels. In those instances when there remains more consecrated wine than was necessary, the ministers shall consume it immediately at a side table before the prayer after Communion, while the vessels themselves may be purified after Mass. The amount of wine to be consecrated should be carefully measured before the celebration so that none remains afterward.
>
> It is strictly prohibited to pour the Precious Blood into the ground or into the sacrarium [HLS 34, 36, 38].

The only time reserving the Precious Blood is allowed is when it is to be used for the Communion of a sick person who is unable to receive the Host.

> The consecrated wine may not be reserved, except for someone who is ill.
>
> Sick people who are unable to receive Communion under the form of bread may receive it under the form of wine alone. If the wine is consecrated at a Mass not celebrated in the presence of the sick person, the Blood of the Lord is kept in a properly covered vessel and is placed in the tabernacle after Communion. The Precious Blood should be carried to the sick in a vessel which is closed in such a way as to eliminate all danger of spilling. If some of the Precious Blood remains, it should be consumed by the minister, who should also see to it that the vessel is properly purified [HLS 37].

For information on the tabernacle—the place where the Eucharist is reserved—see chapter 10.

PRAYER AFTER COMMUNION

After the silence or the song following Communion, or after the purification of the vessels (if this is done during Mass), the priest then invites the faithful to prayer, which closes the Communion rite. The rubrics of the Sacramentary state:

> Then, standing at the chair or at the altar, the priest sings or says: *Let us pray.*
>
> Priest and people pray in silence for a while, unless a period of silence has already been observed. Then the priest extends his hands and sings or says the prayer after Communion, at the end of which the people respond: *Amen.*

9. Concluding Rites

Just as Mass is begun with certain rites, normally it is also brought to a close with certain rites.

The concluding rite consists of:
 a. the priest's greeting and blessing, which on certain days and occasions is expanded and expressed in the prayer over the people or another more solemn formulary;
 b. the dismissal of the assembly, which sends each member back to doing good works, while praising and blessing the Lord [GIRM 57].

The concluding rites do not always occur, however:

If another liturgical service follows Mass, the concluding rites (greeting, blessing, and dismissal) are omitted [GIRM 126].

In most cases, a second liturgical service does not follow, and so the concluding rites take place. They may, however, be *preceded* by parish announcements:

If there are any brief announcements, they may be made at this time [GIRM 123].

If there is a deacon present, he also may make the announcements:

Following the prayer after Communion, if there are any brief announcements, the deacon may make them unless the priest prefers to do them himself [GIRM 139].

The priest then greets and blesses the people:

Then the priest, with hands outstretched, greets the people: *The Lord be with you*. They answer: *And also with you*. The priest immediately adds: *May almighty God bless you* and, as he blesses with the sign of the cross, continues: *the Father, and the Son, and the Holy Spirit*. All answer: *Amen*. On certain days and on certain occasions another, more solemn form of blessing or the prayer over the people precedes this form of blessing as the rubrics direct.

Immediately after the blessing, with hands joined, the priest adds: *Go in the peace of Christ*, or: *Go in peace to love and serve the Lord,* or: *The Mass is ended, go in peace,* and the people answer: *Thanks be to God* [GIRM 124].

If a deacon is present, he may give the dismissal instead of the priest:

After the priest's blessing, the deacon dismisses the people, saying: *Go in the peace of Christ*, or *Go in peace to love and serve the Lord*, or, *The Mass is ended, go in peace* [GIRM 140].

Notice that in the dismissal, the priest or deacon is not required to use just one set of words.

The priest, deacon, and ministers then reverence the altar and leave:

As a rule, the priest then kisses the altar, makes the proper reverence with the ministers, and leaves [GIRM 125].

Along with the priest, the deacon kisses the altar, makes the proper reverence, and leaves in the manner followed for the entrance procession [GIRM 141].

10. Liturgical Furnishings and Vestments

General Considerations

Because of the sacred functions carried out in a church and because it is a place for the public worship and honor of God, it is important that, to the best of the community's ability, the church honor God by its design and furnishings. The same is true of the articles and vestments used in the liturgy itself.

As a result, the Church has laid down some general norms for this area. For example, the *Ceremonial of Bishops* states:

> Vestments, church furnishings, and decorative objects that have been handed down from the past are not to be treated carelessly, but kept in good condition. When anything new needs to be provided, it should be chosen to meet the standards of contemporary art, but not out of a desire for novelty [CB 37].

Often, works of art will be used in the furnishings of a church. These may be freestanding images or paintings or they may be part of some other furnishing. For example, a baptismal font may have a bas-relief carving on its side, depicting a scene or scenes from the Bible. Whether or not art is freestanding or part of another furnishing, the Church is very concerned that it be of the highest quality:

> At all times . . . the Church seeks out the services of the arts and welcomes artistic expressions of all people and regions. The Church is intent on keeping the works of art and the treasure handed down from the past and, when necessary, on adapting

them to new needs. It strives as well to promote new works of art that appeal to the contemporary mentality.

In commissioning artists and choosing works of art that are to become part of a church, the highest standard is therefore to be set, in order that art may aid faith and devotion and be true to the reality it is to symbolize and the purpose it is to serve [GIRM 254].

With this said, we may now look at the regulations the Church provides for specific furnishings and articles.

Baptismal and Holy Water Fonts

A church's baptismal font is also a very important liturgical furnishing, for it is through the sacrament of baptism that people become members of the Church.

The baptistery, or area where the baptismal font is located, should be reserved for the sacrament of baptism and should be worthy to serve as a place where Christians are reborn in water and the Holy Spirit. The baptistery may be situated in a chapel either inside or outside the church or in some part of the church easily seen by the faithful; it should be large enough to accommodate a good number of people.

The baptismal font, or the vessel in which on occasion the water is prepared for the celebration of the sacraments in the sanctuary, should be spotlessly clean and of pleasing design [BC 995].

In some churches, the baptismal font is positioned at the main entrance so that people may dip their fingers in its water and make the sign of the cross, reminding themselves of their entrance into the Church by baptism.

In many churches, however, the baptismal font is located

elsewhere and small holy water fonts take its place at the entrances to the church. The *Ceremonial of Bishops* states:

> It is an old and honored practice for all who enter a church to dip their hand in a font (stoup) of holy water and sign themselves with the sign of the cross as a reminder of their baptism [CB 110].

Following the Mass of the Lord's Supper on Holy Thursday, the fonts are emptied of water until they are refilled with the water blessed at Easter. *Paschales Solemnitatis* states:

> Mass is to be celebrated on Easter Day with great solemnity. It is appropriate that the penitential rite on this day take the form of a sprinkling with water blessed at the Vigil, during which the antiphon *Vidi aquam*, or some other song of baptismal character should be sung. The fonts at the entrance to the church should also be filled with the same water [PS 97].

Candles

Candles play an important role in churches. In the old days they were used as both a source of light and a sign of reverence. Today we now use electric lighting, but candles remain important as a sign of reverence and prayer.

> Candles are to be used at every liturgical service as a sign of reverence and festiveness. The candlesticks are to be placed either on or around the altar in a way suited to the design of the altar and the sanctuary. Everything is to be well balanced and must not interfere with the faithful's clear view of what goes on at the altar or is placed on it [GIRM 269].

Candles or lamps are also used to indicate the reservation of the Eucharist in the tabernacle (see below).

Chairs

During parts of the liturgy, the priest celebrating Mass is directed to sit. Accordingly, the *General Instruction* states:

> The priest celebrant's chair ought to stand as a symbol of his office of presiding over the assembly and the directing of prayer. Thus the best place for the chair is the back of the sanctuary and turned toward the congregation unless the structure or other circumstances are an obstacle (for example, if too great a distance would interfere with the priest and the people.) Anything resembling a throne is to be avoided. The seats for the ministers should be so placed in the sanctuary that they can readily carry out their appointed functions [GIRM 271].

The faithful are also directed to sit during much of the Mass, and so the *General Instruction* makes mention of their seating accommodations as well:

> The places for the faithful should be arranged with care so that the people are able to take their rightful part in the celebration visually and mentally. As a rule, there should be benches or chairs for their use. But the custom of reserving seats for private persons must be abolished. Chairs or benches should be set up in such a way that the people can easily take the positions required during the various celebrations and have unimpeded access to receive Communion [GIRM 273].

Note that the *General Instruction* stresses that the faithful's seats are to be set up so that they can take the different postures—sitting, standing, kneeling—used in the liturgy. We will come back to this in the section on posture in chapter 11.

Images

Though the practice arose much earlier, the Second Council of Nicaea (787) dogmatically defined the liceity of using images of Christ and the saints in church. Since that time images— whether in the forms of mosaics, paintings, stained glass, icons, bas-reliefs, and statuary—have been an ever-present feature of Catholic churches.

This was maintained at the Second Vatican Council:

> The practice of placing sacred images in churches so that they may be venerated by the faithful is to be maintained. Nevertheless there is to be restraint regarding their number and prominence so that they do not create confusion among the Christian people or foster religious practices of doubtful orthodoxy [SC 125].

Correspondingly, the *General Instruction of the Roman Missal* states:

> In keeping with the Church's very ancient tradition, it is lawful to set up in places of worship images of Christ, Mary, and the saints for veneration by the faithful. But there is need both to limit their number and to situate them in such a way that they do not distract the people's attention from the celebration. There is to be only one image of any one saint. In general, the devotion of the entire community is to be the criterion regarding images in the adornment and arrangement of a church [GIRM 278].

Generally there are fewer images displayed in churches now than there were a few decades ago. This is in keeping with the Church's regulations. However, the Church has not in any way mandated a total absence of images or a minimalist approach to their use. From the very beginning of the liturgical reform, concern was shown that images remain a part of Catholic life.

In 1965, Cardinal Giacomo Lercaro, president of the Consilium, wrote a letter to the presidents of the national conferences of bishops in which he stated:

> In the adaptation of churches to the demands of liturgical renewal there has sometimes been exaggeration regarding sacred images. At times, it is true, some churches have been cluttered with images and statues, but to strip bare and do away with absolutely everything is to risk the opposite extreme. [*Le renouveau liturgique*, June 20, 1965; *Notitiae* 1 (1965) 257–264; DOL 417].

The current *Code of Canon Law* is forceful in stating that images *are* to be placed in churches:

CANON 1188

The practice of displaying sacred images in the churches for the veneration of the faithful is to remain in force; nevertheless they are to be exhibited in moderate number and in suitable order lest they bewilder the Christian people and give opportunity for questionable devotion.

The *Code* is also specific about properly preserving images that are treasures from the past:

CANON 1189

Whenever valuable images, that is, those which are outstanding due to age, art, or cult, which are exhibited in churches or oratories for the veneration of the faithful need repair, they are never to be restored without the written permission of the ordinary who is to consult experts before he grants permission.

Musical Instruments

Sometimes the faithful have been horrified by the use of odd musical instruments during Mass which destroys the reverent atmosphere of worship. In some cases, even kazoos and party noisemakers have been used. These are not suitable for use during Mass. Vatican II's Constitution on the Sacred Liturgy states:

> In the Latin Church the pipe organ is to be held in high esteem, for it is the traditional musical instrument that adds a wonderful splendor to the Church's ceremonies and powerfully lifts up the spirit to God and to higher things.
>
> But other instruments also may be admitted for use in divine worship, with the knowledge and consent of the competent territorial authority. . . . This applies, however, only on condition that the instruments are suitable, or can be made suitable, for sacred use, are in accord with the dignity of the place of worship, and truly contribute to the uplifting of the faithful [SC 120].

The Sacred Congregation for Rites further emphasizes this in the instruction *Musicam Sacram*:

> One criterion for accepting and using musical instruments is the genius and traditions of the particular peoples. At the same time, however, instruments that are generally associated and used only with worldly music are to be absolutely barred from liturgical services and religious devotions. All musical instruments accepted for divine worship must be played in such a way as to meet the requirements of a liturgical service and to contribute to the beauty of worship and the building up of the faithful [*Notitiae* 3 (1967) 87–105, 63, DOL 4184].

Accordingly, the U.S. bishops have ruled:

> The Conference of Bishops has decreed that musical instruments other than the organ may be used in liturgical services provided they are played in a manner that is suitable to public worship (November, 1967; see *Constitution on the Liturgy*, art. 120). This decision deliberately refrains from singling out specific instruments. Their use depends on circumstances, the nature of the

congregation, etc. In particular cases, if there should be doubt as to the suitability of the instruments, it is the responsibility of the diocesan bishop, in consultation with the diocesan liturgical and music commissions, to render a decision [AGI 275].

Thus individual priests, liturgical directors, etc., do not make this decision.

It should also be noted that certain styles of music, as well as certain instruments, are prohibited from Mass. For example:

It is necessary, moreover, that the principles of sacredness and dignity which distinguish church music, be it for its chant as for its sound, should remain intact. All that which is merely secular should be proscribed from the house of God. Jazz, for example, cannot today be part of a musical repertoire designed for worship.

Where musical instruments are concerned, differing mentalities, cultures, and traditions are to be borne in mind, and those instruments which have an entirely secular connotation should not be allowed in church. The Church has immense possibilities for deep, effective, and uplifting action, without having recourse to means which are very dubious and even, by common consent, harmful [Notitiae 2 (1966) 157–161, 5, DOL 427].

Altar

Of all the furnishings in a church, the altar is among the most important, because this is where the Eucharistic Sacrifice takes place. Through world history, whether in early Yahwism, in Judaism, in Christianity, or even in non-Christian religions, an altar has always been, in a special way, where man goes to meet and have fellowship with the divine.

On Christian altars, Christ is presented as a living sacrifice to God. He does not suffer or die again, for he did that once for all on the cross. However, the sacrifice of the cross is made sacramentally present on the altar, and in the Eucharist Christ presents himself to the Father as a living sacrifice, just as we are directed to do (Rom. 12:1).

The *General Instruction* states:

> At the altar the sacrifice of the cross is made present under sacramental signs. It is also the table of the Lord and the people of God are called together to share in it. The altar is, as well, the center of the thanksgiving that the Eucharist accomplishes [GIRM 259].

Because of its special importance, the Church makes certain requirements about the construction, maintenance, and use of altars. Among the most important of these is whether an altar is fixed or movable, and where it is to be located. The Code states:

CANON 1235

§1. An altar or a table on which the Eucharistic Sacrifice is celebrated is said to be *fixed* if it is so constructed that it is joined to the floor and therefore cannot be moved; it is *movable* if it can be transferred.

§2. It is fitting that there be a fixed altar in every church; in other places designated for sacred celebration, a fixed altar or a movable altar.

The General Instruction adds:

> In every church there should ordinarily be a fixed, dedicated altar, which should be freestanding to allow the ministers to walk around it easily and Mass to be celebrated facing the people. It should be so placed as to be a focal point on which the attention of the whole congregation centers naturally [GIRM 262].

Also important is the material out of which an altar is made. In the case of a fixed altar, the regulations are more specific:

In accordance with the received custom in the Church and the biblical symbolism connected with an altar, the table of a fixed altar should be of stone, indeed of natural stone. But, at the discretion of the conference of bishops, any becoming, solid and finely wrought material may be used in erecting an altar [CB 919].

The pedestal or base of the table may be of any sort of material, as long as it is becoming and solid [GIRM 263].

However, in the case of a movable altar, more leeway is allowed:

A moveable altar may be constructed of any becoming, solid material suited to liturgical use, according to the traditions and customs of different regions [GIRM 264].

For many centuries, churches typically have had relics of the saints contained under their main altar. This custom remains today:

The practice of placing under the altar to be dedicated relics of saints, even of non-martyrs, is to be maintained. Care must be taken to have solid evidence of the authenticity of such relics [GIRM 266].

The *Code of Canon Law* also mandates this:

CANON 1237 §2

The ancient tradition of keeping the relics of martyrs and other saints under a fixed altar is to be preserved according to the norms given in the liturgical books.

The altar is also to be covered with a special altar cloth:

At least one cloth should be placed on the altar out of reverence for the celebration of the memorial of the Lord and the banquet that gives us his Body and Blood. The shape, size, and decoration of the altar cloth should be in keeping with the design of the altar [GIRM 268].

And, finally, the altar is to be used only in divine worship:

CANON 1239

§1. Both a fixed and a movable altar are to be reserved exclusively for divine worship and entirely exempt from profane use.

§2. No corpse may be buried beneath the altar; otherwise Mass may not be celebrated on it.

Altar Cross

The cross is the most important symbol in Christian history. The *Ceremonial of Bishops* explains:

Of all the sacred images, the "figure of the precious life-giving cross of Christ" is preeminent, because it is the symbol of the entire paschal mystery. The cross is the image most cherished by the Christian people and the most ancient; it represents Christ's suffering and victory, and at the same time, as the Fathers of the Church have taught, it points to his Second Coming [CB 1011].

The cross has historically been associated with the altar because of its preeminence as a Christian symbol and because it represents or depicts the sacrifice of the cross which is made sacramentally present on the altar. However, in recent years some parishioners report that in their churches there is either no cross near the altar or that there is an image of the resurrected Christ instead. Neither of these is permissible. The Church mandates the presence of a cross:

There is also to be a cross, clearly visible to the congregation, either on the altar or near it [GIRM 270].

Only a single cross should be carried in a procession in order to give greater dignity and reverence to the cross. It is desirable to place the cross that has been carried in the procession near the altar so that it may serve as the cross of the altar. Otherwise it should be put away during the service (see Congregation of Rites, Instruction, June 21, 1968, no. 20) [AGI 270].

It should also be noted that this cross, as envisioned in the Church's liturgical documents, is to have a corpus (body of Christ crucified) on it. Msgr. Peter Elliott explains:

The cross should be located on, next to, immediately behind, or suspended above the altar. It ought to be visibly related to the altar as viewed by the people. In the context of the Roman liturgy, "cross" means a crucifix [see Roman Ritual, *Book of Blessings, Blessing of a Cross*, no. 1235]. A figure of the risen Christ behind an altar cannot be regarded as a substitute for the cross. However, there is a wide range of styles of figures to choose from which may be suitable for the liturgical crucifix [CMRR 64].

The section of the Roman Ritual that Msgr. Elliott notes states:

The image of the cross should preferably be a crucifix, that is, have the corpus attached, especially in the case of a cross that is erected in a place of honor inside a church [*Book of Blessings* 1235].

Other places in the Church's liturgical law also assume that a cross will have a corpus on it (e.g., *Ceremonial of Bishops* 128), as indicated by discussions of which direction the cross should be *facing* (e.g., *Notitiae* 2 [1966] 290–291, 101, DOL 386 n. R30).

Since the cross is the place of Christ's *death*, it is odd and inappropriate to depict a risen Christ superimposed on an altar cross. The point of associating a cross with the altar in the first place is that the altar is where Christ's sacrifice is re-presented to God, and his sacrifice—not his resurrection—was done on a cross.

Eucharistic Vessels

The specific vessels used for celebrating the Eucharist are also governed by regulations:

> Among the requisites for the celebration of Mass, the sacred vessels hold a place of honor, especially the chalice and paten, which are used in presenting, consecrating, and receiving the bread and wine.
>
> Vessels should be made from materials that are solid and that in the particular region are regarded as noble. The conference of bishops will be the judge in this matter. But preference is to be given to materials that do not break easily or become unusable [GIRM 289-290].
>
> Vessels made from metal should ordinarily be gilded on the inside if the metal is one that rusts; gilding is not necessary if the metal is more precious than gold and does not rust [GIRM 294].

One class of vessels is those used with the consecrated Hosts:

> Vessels that serve as receptacles for the Eucharistic bread, such as a paten, ciborium, pyx, monstrance, etc., may be made of other materials that are prized in the region, for example, ebony or other hard woods, as long as they are suited to sacred use.
>
> For the consecration of Hosts one rather large paten may properly be used; on it is placed the bread for the priest as well as for the ministers and the faithful [GIRM 292-293].

The paten is typically a flat, dish-like vessel used to hold Hosts—especially the priest's Host—both before and after consecration. It is also used during Communion to prevent

Hosts from dropping to the floor. A ciborium is a vessel that is used to hold many Hosts; it may be shaped either like a chalice or like a dish (one deeper than patens usually are). A pyx is a small container typically used to bring Communion to the sick. It is often shaped like a small, flat, circular box (not unlike a watchcase). A monstrance is a larger Eucharistic vessel used for the exposition and adoration of the Blessed Sacrament.

Typically, such vessels are made from metal; however, as the GIRM reveals, other materials are permitted under certain conditions. Because of abuses in this area, *Inaestimabile Donum* took pains to stress that some materials are *not* appropriate and that the judge of which materials are appropriate is the national conference of bishops and not the individual priest or liturgist:

> Particular respect and care are due to the sacred vessels, both the chalice and paten for the celebration of the Eucharist, and the ciboria for the Communion of the faithful. The form of the vessels must be appropriate for the liturgical use for which they are meant. The material must be noble, durable, and in every case adapted to sacred use. In this sphere, judgment belongs to the episcopal conference of the individual regions.
>
> Use is not to be made of simple baskets or other receptacles meant for ordinary use outside the sacred celebrations, nor are the sacred vessels to be of poor quality or lacking any artistic style.
>
> Before being used, chalices and patens must be blessed by the bishop or by a priest [ID 16].

The other main class of Eucharistic vessels is those associated with the Precious Blood:

> Chalices and other vessels that serve as receptacles for the Blood of the Lord are to have a cup of nonabsorbent material. The base may be of any other solid and worthy material [GIRM 291].

The Holy See has also stressed the use of a veil for the chalice:

Query: In a great many places the veil is hardly ever used to cover the chalice prepared at a side table before Mass. Have any recent norms been given to suppress use of the veil?

Reply: There is no norm, not even a recent one, to change the GIRM no. 80c, which reads: "The chalice should be covered with a veil, which may always be white" [*Notitiae* 14 (1978) 594, no. 16, 1470].

Tabernacle

One of the most controversial issues concerning liturgical furnishings is the proper placement of the tabernacle in which the Eucharist is reserved. Sometimes individuals in parishes insist on moving the tabernacle on the basis of the previously discussed document, *Environment and Art in Catholic Worship* (see the section in chapter 1 on the Church's liturgical documents).

Section 78 of the document states that the tabernacle should be placed in a separate chapel. However, this document has no legal authority (see the section on the Church's liturgical documents in chapter 1). Neither the National Conference of Catholic Bishops nor the Holy See ratified it, and the approval of *both* would be required to give it authority.

Msgr. Peter J. Elliott, noted author of the guidebook *Ceremonies of the Modern Roman Rite*, suggests the reason for the document's recommendation concerning the placement of the tabernacle:

A partial reading of authorities and consequent dogmatism is evident in *Environment and Art in Catholic Worship*, 1978, nos. 78, 79. To be fair to the authors, their opinions reflect the era of the 1970s and were presented before *Inaestimabile Donum* and the new Code. But this dated document continues to circulate, endorsed and unmodified [CMRR 325, n. 1].

Inaestimabile Donum, which the Holy See released after *Environment and Art* and which carries authority from the Holy See, has a very different attitude toward the placement of the tabernacle:

> The tabernacle in which the Eucharist is kept can be located on an altar, or away from it, in a spot in the church which is very prominent, truly noble, and duly decorated, or in a chapel suitable for private prayer and for adoration by the faithful [ID 24].

The *Code of Canon Law* states:

CANON 938

§1. The Most Holy Eucharist is to be reserved regularly in only one tabernacle of a church or oratory.

§2. The tabernacle in which the Most Holy Eucharist is reserved should be placed in a part of the church that is prominent, conspicuous, beautifully decorated, and suitable for prayer.

One of the troubles with many Eucharistic adoration chapels is that they are *not* conspicuous and in a prominent place in the church, but hidden, out of the way, and not easily accessible, in spite of canon 938 §2. Sometimes even a *closet* has been converted into a "side chapel" for Jesus!

For an excellent and thorough discussion of the placement of the tabernacle and how the Church's regulations concerning it have developed over time (to the most recent authoritative statement found in the Code, above), see Appendix 9 of *Ceremonies of the Modern Roman Rite*.

In addition to the location of the tabernacle, the Church also mandates certain other things concerning it. *Inaestimabile Donum* stated:

> The tabernacle should be solid, unbreakable, and not transparent. The presence of the Eucharist is to be indicated by a taber-

nacle veil or by some other suitable means laid down by the competent authority, and a lamp must perpetually burn before it, as a sign of honor paid to the Lord [ID 25].

In the same vein, the *Code of Canon Law* states:

CANON 938 §3

The tabernacle in which the Eucharist is regularly reserved is to be immovable, made of solid and opaque material, and locked so that the danger of profanation may be entirely avoided.

Finally, many have asked whether the practice of genuflecting before the tabernacle is to be maintained. The answer is yes:

The venerable practice of genuflecting before the Blessed Sacrament, whether enclosed in the tabernacle or publicly exposed, as a sign of adoration, is to be maintained. This act requires that it be performed in a recollected way. In order that the heart may bow before God in profound reverence, the genuflection must be neither hurried nor careless [ID 26].

Liturgical Vestments

The wearing of special clothing for ministering at a liturgy has roots going back thousands of years. It is mentioned, for example, in Exodus 28, where the Lord tells Moses:

Make sacred garments for your brother Aaron, to give him dignity and honor. Tell all the skilled men to whom I have given wisdom in such matters that they are to make garments for Aaron, for his consecration, so he may serve me as priest [Ex. 28:2-3].

This practice is still honored today. The *General Instruction* states:

In the Church, the Body of Christ, not all members have the same function. This diversity of ministries is shown outwardly in worship by the diversity of vestments. These should therefore symbolize the function proper to each ministry. But at the same time the vestments should also contribute to the beauty of the rite [GIRM 297].

Not all vestments are suitable, however, and so attention must be paid to their design and to the materials of which they are made:

Regarding the design of vestments, the conferences of bishops may determine and propose to the Apostolic See adaptations that correspond to the needs and usages of their regions.

In addition to the traditional materials, natural fabrics proper to the region may be used for making vestments; artificial fabrics that are in keeping with the dignity of the liturgy and the person wearing them may also be used. The conference of bishops will be the judge in this matter.

The beauty of a vestment should derive from its material and design rather than from lavish ornamentation. Representations on vestments should consist only of symbols, images, or pictures portraying the sacred. Anything out of keeping with the sacred is to be avoided [GIRM 304–306].

Types of Vestments

The discussion of what constitutes proper liturgical vestments is complicated because many people are unfamiliar with the proper terms for vestments. Therefore, we present the following definitions:

Alb. A long-sleeved white linen robe that reaches the ankles. It is worn by ministers of the altar over their other garb and may be decorated in a variety of ways.

Amice. A rectangular piece of linen with two long strips attached to two of its corners. It is worn under the alb and is optional if the alb is made in such a way as to cover the wearer's street clothing at the neck.

Chasuble. The outermost vestment of the celebrating priest at Mass and reflecting the liturgical color of the day or season. Though different styles have been used, the most common today is that of a large piece of cloth with a hole in the center for the priest's head.

Cincture. A cord used to gather the alb at the waist. May be white or the liturgical color of the day.

Cope. A floor-length vestment resembling a cloak. It is worn at various rites, including Eucharistic Benediction, and is usually highly decorated.

Cowl. A hood or hooded robe worn by monks and other men religious.

Dalmatic. A tunic of varying lengths and decorative style that is worn over other liturgical vestments, especially by deacons. It reflects the liturgical color of the day.

Stole. A long strip of cloth worn around the neck as a symbol of office by a bishop, priest, or deacon. Its color matches the liturgical color of the day.

Surplice. A loose-fitting vestment made of cotton or linen that typically reaches just below the hips. Often worn by laymen over a cassock when serving at liturgies.

Some of these vestments are based on clothing that was common in ancient times but which has been replaced in secular society. The alb, for example, is based on a Greco-Roman tunic, the chasuble on a tunic cover, and the cope from a Roman raincoat. Due to the dignified nature of liturgy, these forms of clothing retained their use at Mass (although in a developed form) when their secular counterparts fell out of fashion. This is similar to how, on formal occasions in our society, dignified clothing is worn that used to be common in secular society but which is now out of fashion except on these occasions (e.g., top hats and long coattails).

Use of Vestments

In some areas, priests' wearing minimal vestments, such as a stole over plainly visible street clothes—even shorts—has disturbed parishioners. The Congregation for Divine Worship forbade this practice in its liturgical instruction of September 5, 1970:

> The vestment common to ministers of every rank is the alb. The abuse is here repudiated of celebrating or even concelebrating Mass with stole only over the monastic cowl or over ordinary clerical garb, to say nothing of street clothes. Equally forbidden is the wearing of the stole alone over street clothes when carrying out other ritual acts, for example, the laying on of hands at ordinations, administering the other sacraments, giving blessings [*Notitiae* 7 (1971) 10–26, 8c, DOL 526].

The recent instruction on collaboration stresses that the ordained must wear *all* the liturgical vestments prescribed for them and that the faithful may wear *only* those liturgical vestments proper to them in the roles that they fulfill at Mass:

> In the same way, the use of sacred vestments which are reserved to priests or deacons (stoles, chasubles or dalmatics) at liturgical ceremonies by non-ordained members of the faithful is clearly unlawful.
>
> Every effort must be made to avoid even the appearance of confusion which can spring from anomalous liturgical practices.

As the sacred ministers are obliged to wear all of the prescribed liturgical vestments so too the non-ordained faithful may not assume that which is not proper to them [ICP, Practical Provisions 6 §2].

The *General Instruction* offers a more thorough discussion of liturgical vestments. It also affirms that the most basic vestment worn by different kinds of ministers (priests, deacons, acolytes, etc.) is the alb:

> The vestment common to ministers of every rank is the alb, tied at the waist with a cincture, unless it is made to fit without a cincture. An amice should be put on first if the alb does not completely cover the street clothing at the neck. A surplice may not be substituted for the alb when the chasuble or dalmatic is to be worn or when a stole is used instead of the chasuble or dalmatic [GIRM 298].

The priest who is celebrating Mass normally is to wear a chasuble:

> Unless otherwise indicated, the chasuble, worn over the alb and stole, is the vestment proper to the priest celebrant at Mass and other rites immediately connected with Mass [GIRM 299].

The *Ceremonial of Bishops* describes the priest's vestment in this way:

> Unless otherwise indicated, the chasuble, worn over the alb and stole, is the vestment proper to the presbyter who is the celebrant at Mass and at other rites immediately connected with Mass.
>
> The priest wears the stole around his neck and hanging down in front.
>
> The cope is worn by the priest in solemn liturgical services outside the Mass and in the processions; in other liturgical services, in keeping with the rubrics proper to each rite.

Presbyters who take part in a liturgical service but not as concelebrants are to wear choir dress if they are prelates or canons, cassocks and surplice if they are not [CB 66].

Priests who are concelebrating with the principal celebrant may wear a chasuble over their stole, but not always:

In the sacristy or other suitable place, the concelebrants put on the vestments usual for individual celebrations. For a good reason, however, as when there are more concelebrants than vestments, the concelebrants may omit the chasuble and simply wear the stole over their alb; but the principal celebrant always wears the chasuble [GIRM 160].

In special situations, a priest may also wear a cope:

The cope is worn by the priest in processions and other services, in keeping with the rubrics proper to each rite [GIRM 303].

Deacons are to be vested somewhat differently than priests. The *Ceremonial of Bishops* explains:

The dalmatic, worn over the alb and stole, is the vestment proper to the deacon. The dalmatic may be omitted either out of necessity or for less solemnity. The deacon wears the stole over his left shoulder and drawn across the chest to the right side, where it is fastened [CB 67].

For both the priest and the deacon, the stole serves as a sign of their ordination. The stole reflects different levels of holy orders that they have received:

The priest wears the stole around his neck and hanging down in front. The deacon wears it over his left shoulder and drawn across the chest to the right side, where it is fastened [GIRM 302].

The Holy See indicated that wearing a stole during Mass is mandatory:

Query: May the priest omit wearing the stole?

Reply: No. The query arises from an interpretation of the GIRM no. 299. The contents of that number, "The chasuble is the vestment proper to the priest celebrant, at Masses and other rites . . . ," must be understood as governed by nos. 81 and 302. From these it is altogether clear that the stole is a priestly vestment that never is to be left off at Mass and other rites directly connected with Mass [*Notitiae* 6 (1970) 104, no. 30, DOL 1689 n. R53].

Non-ordained ministers (those who are not bishops, priests, or deacons) typically wear the alb:

Ministers below the order of deacon may wear the alb or other vestment that is lawfully approved in each region [GIRM 301].

One final note: Some have inquired about the appropriate vestment for extraordinary ministers of Holy Communion. Regarding this issue, the Holy See has said,

The [extraordinary] minister who is to distribute Communion is to wear either the liturgical vestment in use locally or clothing befitting this sacred ministry [*Notitiae* 9 (1973) 167, DOL 2951].

For a mainstream American parish, this excludes tee-shirts, beach wear, tank tops, shorts, miniskirts, unkempt clothing, and other secular or suggestive clothing that mainstream American culture does not regard as suitable for fulfilling sacred functions.

No distinction is made in this between the vestment of male and female extraordinary ministers. If the alb is used locally as the vestment for male extraordinary ministers, then it may be used by female extraordinary ministers, too.

PROPER COLORS FOR VESTMENTS

The issue of the appropriate colors for liturgical vestments has also been of concern in many areas. Liturgical colors are not unimportant; they have a specific purpose in the life of the Church. The *General Instruction* explains:

> Variety in the color of the vestments is meant to give effective, outward expression to the specific character of the mysteries of the faith being celebrated and, in the course of the year, to a sense of progress in the Christian life [GIRM 307].

The *General Instruction* mandates that the following colors be used:

> Traditional usage should be retained for the vestment colors.
>
> a. White is used in the offices and Masses of the Easter and Christmas seasons; on feasts and memorials of the Lord, other than of his passion; on feasts and memorials of Mary, the angels, saints who were not martyrs, All Saints (1 November), John the Baptist (24 June), John the Evangelist (27 December), the Chair of Saint Peter (22 February), and the Conversion of Saint Paul (25 January).
>
> b. Red is used on Passion Sunday (Palm Sunday) and Good Friday, Pentecost, celebrations of the Lord's passion, birthday feasts of the apostles and evangelists, and celebrations of martyrs.
>
> c. Green is used in the offices and Masses of Ordinary Time.
>
> d. Violet is used in Lent and Advent. It may also be worn in offices and Masses for the dead.
>
> e. Black may be used in Masses for the dead.
>
> f. Rose may be used on Gaudete Sunday (third Sunday of Advent) and Laetare Sunday (fourth Sunday of Lent).
>
> The conference of bishops may choose and propose to the Apostolic See adaptations suited to the needs and culture of peoples [GIRM 308].

The American *Appendix to the General Instruction* adds:

> White, violet, or black vestments may be worn at funeral services and at other offices and Masses for the dead (November, 1970) [AGI 308].

There are some occasions when an approved liturgical color other than the one listed for a given day may be used:

> On solemn occasions more precious vestments may be used, even if not of the color of the day [GIRM 309].

The appropriate liturgical color also may be affected by the type of Mass being celebrated:

> Ritual Masses are celebrated in their proper color, in white, or in a festive color; Masses for various needs and occasions are celebrated in the color proper to the day or the season or in violet if they bear a penitential character, for example, ritual Masses nos. 23, 28, and 40; votive Masses are celebrated in the color suited to the Mass itself or in the color proper to the day or season [GIRM 310].

Some have asked about the practice of priests wearing *blue* vestments during Advent and Lent instead of purple. While wearing a blue-*ish* purple would not be proscribed, pure blue is not permitted. Lent and Advent are penitential seasons, and purple is the authorized color for them. Blue is *not* the same color as purple, even though they are next to each other on the color spectrum, and the use of blue as a color for vestments has *not* been authorized for the Latin Rite in the United States. A priest or even an individual bishop cannot change this on his own authority.

11. Liturgical Postures and Actions

Just as there are certain prayers that are proper to the ordained and other prayers that are proper to the laity, so there are certain postures and actions that are proper to the ordained and others that are proper to the laity. This was stressed in the recent instruction on collaboration between the laity and the priesthood. After indicating that certain prayers of the Mass are reserved to priests, it states:

> Neither may deacons or non-ordained members of the faithful use gestures or actions which are proper to the same priest celebrant. It is a grave abuse for any member of the non-ordained faithful to "quasi-preside" at the Mass while leaving only that minimal participation to the priest which is necessary to secure validity [ICP, Practical Provisions 6 §2].

Fortunately, cases where members of the laity "quasi-preside" are rare—usually only found at conferences held by dissidents. However, there are many cases where the laity assume postures proper to the priest (such as standing when they are supposed to be kneeling) or use gestures proper to the priest (such as praying with arms outstretched).

Posture During Mass

Currently, one of the most controversial topics on which liturgical abuses occur is posture—and especially kneeling—during

Mass. There is a lot of confusion over when one should or should not be standing, sitting, or kneeling. Yet the rules are quite simple.

The *General Instruction of the Roman Missal* establishes the worldwide norms for posture. These are adapted, with approval of the Holy See, in particular countries. Here we present what the *General Instruction* states and adaptations approved by the Holy See for the United States, as found in the American *Appendix to the General Instruction*.

STANDING

The worldwide norm is this:

> Unless other provision is made, at every Mass the people should stand from the beginning of the entrance song or when the priest enters until the end of the opening prayer or collect; for the singing of the *Alleluia* before the Gospel; while the Gospel is being proclaimed; during the profession of faith and the general intercessions; from the prayer over the gifts to the end of the Mass, except at the places indicated . . . [GIRM 21].

The American usage is identical except the period from after the *Sanctus* to after the Great Amen, where additional kneeling is mandated (see below).

In some places, especially where there is a very small congregation in attendance, the priest invites the members of the congregation (or some of them, such as teenagers in a Mass for teens) to stand with him around the altar during the Eucharistic prayer. The Holy See has given the following ruling on this practice:

> *Query: At the presentation of gifts at a Mass with congregation, persons (lay or religious) bring to the altar the bread and wine which are to be consecrated. These gifts are received by the priest celebrant. All those*

participating in the Mass accompany this group procession in which the gifts are brought forward. They then stand around the altar until Communion time. Is this procedure in conformity with the spirit of the law and of the Roman Missal?

Reply: Assuredly, the Eucharistic celebration is the act of the entire community, carried out by all the members of the liturgical assembly. Nevertheless, everyone must have and also must observe his or her own place and proper role: "In liturgical celebrations each one, minister or layperson, who has an office to perform, should do all of, but only, those parts which pertain to that office by the nature of the rite and the principles of liturgy" [SC art. 29].

During the liturgy of the Eucharist, only the presiding celebrant remains at the altar. The assembly of the faithful take their place in the Church outside the *presbyterium*, which is reserved for the celebrant or concelebrants and altar ministers [*Notitiae* 17 (1981) 61].

Sitting

The worldwide norm is this:

[The people] should sit during the readings before the Gospel and during the responsorial psalm, for the homily and the presentation of the gifts, and, if this seems helpful, during the period of silence after Communion [GIRM 21].

The American usage is identical.

Kneeling

The worldwide norm is this:

[The people] should kneel at the consecration unless prevented by the lack of space, the number of people, or some other good reason [GIRM 21].

The American adaptation is as follows:

At its meeting in November, 1969, the National Conference of Catholic Bishops voted that in general, the directives of the *Roman Missal* concerning the posture of the congregation at Mass should be left unchanged, but that no. 21 of the *General Instruction* should be adapted so that the people kneel beginning after the singing or recitation of the *Sanctus* until after the Amen of the Eucharistic Prayer, that is, before the Lord's prayer [AGI 21].

This means that in the United States people are to kneel *after* the *Sanctus* ("Holy, Holy, Holy . . .") and remain kneeling until *after* the Amen of the Eucharistic Prayer, also known as the Great Amen, which follows the priest's *Per Ipsum* ("Through him, with him, in him . . .").

People are not to stand up *before* the Great Amen, nor are to they stand up *during* the Great Amen. The Great Amen is the climax of the congregation's participation in the Eucharistic Prayer, when it solemnly assents, as a body, to what the priest has just prayed to God as their representative. This special solemnity is why, in America, the congregation remains kneeling *during* the Amen. Standing before the Amen is not permitted, and it is especially inappropriate to be changing postures *during* this most solemn moment.

In many parishes in America it is also customary to kneel during the second elevation of the Host, when the priest says *This is the Lamb of God who takes away the sins of the world. Happy are those who are called to his supper,* and the people respond *Lord, I am not worthy to receive you, but only say the word and I shall be healed.* The rubrics do not specify kneeling at this point. Therefore, it is not a liturgical abuse for a priest to ask the congregation to remain standing during this, in accordance with the rubrics and the worldwide practice.

The subject of one's posture when receiving Communion has also been controversial, but the Holy See has ruled:

With regard to the manner of going to Communion, the faithful can receive it either kneeling or standing, in accordance with the norms laid down by the episcopal conference: When the faithful communicate kneeling, no other sign of reverence towards the Blessed Sacrament is required, since kneeling is itself a sign of adoration. When they receive Communion standing, it is strongly recommended that, coming up in procession, they should make a sign of reverence before receiving the Sacrament. This should be done at the right time and place, so that the order of people going to and from Communion is not disrupted [ID 11].

Regarding posture *after* receiving Communion, the Holy See has given the following reply:

Query: After Communion should the faithful be seated or not?

Reply: After Communion they may either kneel, stand, or sit. Accordingly the GIRM no. 21 gives this rule: "The people sit . . . if this seems useful during the period of silence after Communion." Thus it is a matter of option, not obligation. The GIRM no. 121, should, therefore, be interpreted to match no. 21 [*Notitiae* 10 (1974) 407, DOL 1411 n. R2].

Many people ask about the law concerning the presence of kneelers for the pews in their parishes. Church law does not require the presence of kneelers, but it *does* require the practice of kneeling. It is simply a question of how comfortable the parish wants to make the parishioners while they kneel in accordance with the Church's liturgical law. The Holy See has ruled that the absence of kneelers is *not* a sufficient reason to remain standing or sitting:

Query: In some places kneelers have been taken out of the churches. Thus, the people can only stand or sit and this detracts from the reverence and adoration due to the Eucharist.

Reply: The appointments of a place of worship have some relationship to the customs of the particular locale. For example, in the East there are carpets; in the Roman basilicas, only since modern times, there are usually chairs without kneelers, so as to accommodate large crowds. There is nothing to prevent the faithful from kneeling on the floor to show their adoration, no matter how uncomfortable this may be. In cases where kneeling is not possible (see GIRM no. 21), a deep bow and a respectful bearing are signs of the reverence and adoration to be shown at the time of the consecration and Communion [*Notitiae* 14 (1978) 302–303, no. 4, DOL 1411 n. R2].

Finally, though kneelers are not mentioned, the Church does state that the places where the faithful sit should be set up so that people can easily assume the different postures the liturgy requires.

Chairs or benches should be set up in such a way that the people can easily take the positions required during the various celebrations and have unimpeded access to receive Communion [GIRM 273].

Thus it is not appropriate to leave out kneelers and jam the chairs or pews so close together that it is impossible to kneel.

Acts of Reverence

GENUFLECTIONS

Genuflecting is a way of showing reverence that has been an important part of Christian ritual for centuries. The *Ceremonial of Bishops* explains it this way:

A genuflection, made by bending only the right knee to the ground, signifies adoration, and is therefore reserved for the

Blessed Sacrament, whether exposed or reserved in the tabernacle, and for the holy cross from the time of the solemn adoration in the liturgical celebration of Good Friday until the beginning of the Easter Vigil [CB 69].

The priest is called upon to genuflect at specific points during the liturgy of the Eucharist:

Three genuflections are made [by the priest] during Mass: After the showing of the Eucharistic bread, after the showing of the chalice, and before Communion.

If there is a tabernacle with the Blessed Sacrament in the sanctuary, a genuflection is made before and after Mass and whenever anyone passes in front of the Blessed Sacrament [GIRM 233].

The laity are also called upon to genuflect:

No one who enters a church should fail to adore the Blessed Sacrament either by visiting the Blessed Sacrament chapel or at least by genuflecting.

Similarly, those who pass before the Blessed Sacrament genuflect, except when they are walking in procession [CB 71].

This requirement is reflected in *Inaestimabile Donum* as well:

The venerable practice of genuflecting before the Blessed Sacrament, whether enclosed in the tabernacle or publicly exposed, as a sign of adoration, is to be maintained. This act requires that it be performed in a recollected way. In order that the heart may bow before God in profound reverence, the genuflection must be neither hurried nor careless [ID 26].

An exception to the requirement to genuflect is made for those who are carrying articles, especially if they are in procession:

Neither a genuflection nor a deep bow is made by those who are carrying articles used in a celebration, for example, the cross, candlesticks, the Book of the Gospels [CB 70].

Bows

Another traditional way of expressing reverence is the bow. The *Ceremonial of Bishops* explains:

> A bow signifies reverence and honor toward a person or toward objects that represent persons.
>
> There are two kinds of bows, a bow of the head and a bow of the body:
>
> a. A bow of the head is made at the name of Jesus, the Blessed Virgin Mary, the saint in whose honor the Mass or the liturgy of hours is being celebrated;
>
> b. A bow of the body, or deep bow, is made: to the altar if there is no tabernacle with the Blessed Sacrament on the altar; to the bishop, before and after incensation, as indicated in no. 91; whenever it is expressly called for by the rubrics of the various liturgical books [CB 68].

Priests, deacons, and ministers are called upon to make deep bows at several points in the liturgy, as indicated in the rubrics. However, the laity are also required to make a deep bow at certain points.

> A deep bow is made to the altar by all who enter the sanctuary (chancel), leave it, or pass before the altar [CB 72].

As noted above, in the section on genuflecting, a deep bow or bow of the body is not made by those carrying articles for use in the Mass.

One bow the laity makes that calls for special attention occurs during the profession of faith, where the rubrics state:

> All bow during these two lines:
>
> *by the power of the Holy Spirit*
> *he was born of the Virgin Mary, and became man.*

As noted, on certain days during the year there is to be a genuflection at the words *and became man*.

At some Masses, people seem to begin the bow too late, but since its purpose is to commemorate the Incarnation of Christ, it is important to have the bow begin at the proper time.

Kiss

A kiss is a traditional sign of greeting and reverence that goes back in Christian history to the days of the apostles. Thus Saint Paul tells his readers, "Greet one another with a holy kiss" (Rom. 16:16, 1 Cor. 16:20, 2 Cor. 13:12) or to "Greet all the brethren with a holy kiss" (1 Thess. 5:26), and Saint Peter states: "Greet one another with the kiss of love" (1 Peter 5:14).

This is the basis of the sign of peace during Mass, though since kissing is not as universally used as a greeting in our culture, other, more common greetings, such as handshakes, are typically used instead. However, kissing as a sign of reverence does still have a place in the Mass, as priests and deacons are directed to kiss the altar and the Book of the Gospels:

> In addition, the celebrant and the concelebrants at the beginning of Mass kiss the altar as a sign of reverence. The principal celebrant as a rule venerates the altar as a sign of reverence. The principal celebrant as a rule venerates the altar by kissing it before he leaves while the other concelebrants, particularly if there is a number of them, venerate the altar by bowing.
>
> When the bishop presides at a solemn celebration of morning or evening prayer, he kisses the altar at the beginning and, as circumstances suggest, at the end.
>
> But if such a sign of reverence as kissing the altar is out of keeping with the traditions of the culture of the region, the conference of bishops may substitute some other sign, after informing the Apostolic See [CB 73].

Praying with Arms Outstretched

One final gesture of reverence is praying with arms outstretched, which is the traditional posture of prayer for priests and bishops during the liturgy:

> Customarily in the Church a bishop or presbyter addresses prayers to God while standing and with hands slightly raised and outstretched.
>
> This practice appears already in the tradition of the Old Testament, and was taken over by Christians in memory of the Lord's passion: "Not only do we raise our hands, but we hold them outstretched so that by imitating the Lord in his passion, we bear witness to him as we pray" [CB 104, citing Tertullian, *De Oratione*, 14].

The U.S. Bishops have considered permitting the laity to mimic these gestures of the priest or bishop, but the Holy See has not approved this, and the more recent instruction on collaboration prohibits the laity from mimicking the gestures appropriate to a priest (see the introduction to the current chapter).

Liturgical Dancing

In 1975, the Congregation for the Sacraments and Divine Worship prepared a document titled *Religious Dance, An Expression of Spiritual Joy* (*Notitiae* 11 [1975] 202–205), which it described as a "qualified and authoritative sketch" of the subject and said it was to be considered "an authoritative point of reference for every discussion on the matter."

Although the document noted that religious dance plays a positive role in many cultures,

> [D]ance has never been made an integral part of the official worship of the Latin Church. If local churches have accepted the

dance, sometimes even in the church building, that was on the occasion of feasts in order to manifest sentiments of joy and devotion. But that always took place outside of liturgical services. Conciliar decisions have often condemned the religious dance because it conduces little to worship and because it could degenerate into disorder.

The document also names a number of specific cultures where religious dance plays or has played a role in the liturgy:

Concretely: There are cultures in which this is possible insofar as dancing is still reflective of religious values and becomes a clear manifestation of them. Such is the case of the Ethiopians. In their culture, even today, there is the religious ritualized dance, clearly distinct from the martial dance and from the amorous dance. The ritual dance is performed by priests and levites before beginning a ceremony and in the open air in front of the church. The dance accompanies the chanting of psalms during the procession. When the procession enters the church, then the chanting of the psalms is carried out with and accompanied by bodily movement.

The same thing is found in the Syriac liturgy by means of chanting of psalms.

In the Byzantine Liturgy, there is an extremely simplified dance on the occasion of a wedding when the crowned spouses make a circular revolution around the lectern together with the celebrant.

Such is the case of the Israelites: In the synagogue their prayer is accompanied by a continuous movement to recall the precept from tradition: "When you pray, do so with all your heart, and all your bones." And for primitive peoples the same observation can be made.

But the document is forceful in stating that this does not mean religious dance can be used in the liturgy in Western culture:

However, the same criterion and judgment cannot be applied in the western culture.

Here dancing is tied with love, with diversion, with profaneness, with unbridling of the senses: Such dancing, in general, is not pure.

For that reason it cannot be introduced into liturgical celebrations of any kind whatever: that would be to inject into the liturgy one of the most desacralized and desacralizing elements; and so it would be equivalent to creating an atmosphere of profaneness which would easily recall to those present and to the participants in the celebration worldly places and situations.

In some places a kind of pseudo-ballet or "interpretive dance" has been tried in liturgy, but the document indicates this is equally prohibited:

Neither can acceptance be had of the proposal to introduce into the liturgy the so-called artistic ballet because there would be presentation here also of a spectacle at which one would assist, while in the liturgy one of the norms from which one cannot prescind is that of participation.

Therefore, there is a great difference in cultures: what is well received in one culture cannot be taken on by another culture.

The traditional reserve of the seriousness of religious worship, and of the Latin worship in particular, must never be forgotten.

This does not mean that religious dance cannot be done at all. It can be done, but only when three conditions are met: (1) that it not take place during the liturgy (e.g., not during Mass), (2) that it not take place in strictly liturgical areas (e.g., in the sanctuary or nave of a church), and (3) that priests do not participate in the religious dance. The document specifies:

If the proposal of the religious dance in the West is really to be made welcome, care will have to be taken that in its regard a place be found *outside of the liturgy*, in *assembly areas which are not strictly liturgical.* Moreover, the priests *must always be excluded* from the dance [emphasis added].

In 1994 the Holy See reiterated:

Among some *peoples*, singing is instinctively accompanied by handclapping, rhythmic swaying, and dance movements on the part of the participants. Such forms of external expression can have a place in the liturgical actions of *these peoples* on condition that they are always the expression of true communal prayer of adoration, praise, offering and supplication, and not simply a performance [*Instruction on Inculturation and the Roman Liturgy,* 42; emphasis added].

12. Practical Steps

Previous chapters have been intended as a resource for both priests and laity. This chapter, however, is intended primarily for laity who encounter liturgical abuses and are at a loss for how to deal with them.

How to Deal with Liturgical Abuses

When responding to a liturgical abuse, one should follow a definite sequence of steps:

1. PRAY FOR GUIDANCE AND FOR A SPIRIT OF HUMILITY AND LOVE

Liturgical abuse is a complex and important subject that has the potential to stir up strong, unpleasant emotions on both sides. For these reasons, whenever one is confronting a situation in which one believes a liturgical abuse may exist, one should always pray for guidance in determining whether there is an abuse and, if so, what to do about it.

To avoid the hostile and painful emotions that discussing liturgical abuses can stir up, one should also pray that one will maintain a spirit of humility and love toward all who are involved in the situation. One must determine that one *will* approach others with these attitudes, and one should pray that they would also respond in a humble and loving way.

2. DETERMINE WHETHER A LITURGICAL ABUSE IS ACTUALLY OCCURRING

Often people run into situations in which a priest, deacon, or minister is doing something which they do not like, but which is not actually a liturgical abuse (a violation of the Church's liturgical law). Before making an issue of a practice, one must first determine whether an abuse is being committed—and the test for that is *not our personal preferences* but the Church's liturgical law.

In many instances, one finds liturgical practices that are unsettling or displeasing but which do not violate any norms or which are actually provided as an option. With the potential pitfalls of damaging one's credibility and creating consternation with clergy and parishioners, one must conduct individual research or secure the assistance of experts in the field before attempting to correct perceived problems.

Many of the Church's laws and regulations that pertain to liturgical abuses are discussed in this book. However, there is no substitute for consulting the original sources or for obtaining the counsel of experts. For information on obtaining these and investigating possible liturgical abuses not mentioned in this book, consult the "Where to Go for More Help" section below and follow its instructions carefully.

3. DETERMINE WHETHER TO TAKE ACTION CONCERNING THE ABUSE

Although any liturgical abuse is a violation of one's rights, sometimes one needs to be humble and, out of Christian charity, allow one's rights to be violated. I generally advise people that they should not make an issue of minor abuses, unless they have a good rapport with the person that would allow them to point out minor things without offending him or making him angry.

If one does not have that special rapport, it is important to engage him only over major liturgical abuses—for the very practical reason that one has only a limited number of "bullets" to shoot before one is branded as a "troublemaker" in the parish. Once that happens, the chance of getting an abuse corrected diminishes, and one's relationship with the person may be poisoned, with negative spiritual effects on both parties. It may also be important to save one's "bullets" in case serious theological problems arise, rather than for liturgical abuses. The former normally are worse than the latter, though not always.

In deciding whether to take action concerning a liturgical abuse, one must weigh, among other things, whether more harm or good will be done by bringing it up. We must decide to act, not based simply on the fact that we are right and that an abuse should not continue, but based on whether our taking action will help or harm the local church.

In the case of very serious abuses (e.g., use of invalid matter for the Eucharist), the benefit to the parish dictates that something must be done (e.g., because it is not a valid Eucharist and the people are not receiving and adoring Jesus Christ). However, in the case of minor liturgical abuses, it may cause more harm than good to try to get them corrected. Only those with personal knowledge of the parish, the people in it, and the type of abuse being committed will be able to determine whether action should or should not be taken, though one should also consider consulting the organizations mentioned below in the "Where to Go for More Help" section.

4. APPROACH THE PERSON COMMITTING THE ABUSE

If one does decide to take action concerning the liturgical abuse, one usually should begin by speaking to the person doing it, whether that person is a lector, extraordinary minister of Holy Communion, deacon, priest, or pastor. One generally does not *begin* by going over someone's head. That is not only less likely to produce results, it can reveal a defect in Christian charity, which always seeks to cure a problem on the lowest level possible and with the least amount of stress possible (cf. Matt. 18:15–17). In general, only if the abuse is not corrected *and* one determines that it is worth pursuing it further should one move up the chain of authority.

When approaching the person, it is important to be as respectful and friendly as possible. Not only will this increase the chances of having the abuse corrected, it is necessary in Christian charity. One should also try to be as relaxed and non-threatening as possible.

One might try sending a one-page letter to the person to request that the abuse be corrected.

If it can be done in a non-threatening way, consider giving the person a copy of this book as a gift and indicating the specific area you would like him to examine.

If there is no specific area, tell him that you didn't have anything in particular in mind, but that you thought he might like it as a reference work for his personal library (otherwise he may not know what to think and assume you are making some kind of general indictment of his way of carrying out his ministry, something you must strenuously avoid).

If one is talking to a priest, it is especially important to be respectful, polite, and friendly. Not only for the reasons stated above, but also because priests deserve special honor by virtue of their ordination and station in the Church. One should speak to a priest as kindly as one would when correcting one's own father (cf. 1 Tim. 5:1).

One should also approach him with specific documentation showing where in the Church's liturgical law the abuse is prohibited. One should not say, "What you are doing is wrong." It would be better to say, "Here (in this quotation from an official text), it says that the practice is not allowed. Is there a more recent ruling you can show me, and, if not, could we do it this way?"

Following the advice of Matthew 18:15–17, one might initially approach the priest alone and, if he does not respond to the request to have the abuse corrected, one should then take a few others from the congregation to ask for it to be corrected. This will make him aware that the matter is of concern to more than one person in the congregation and should be taken more seriously.

5. APPEAL TO HIGHER AUTHORITY

Only if these efforts fail should one go over the priest's head and talk to the pastor of the parish, and only if that fails should one appeal still higher. If the pastor of the parish is unresponsive then one may consider speaking to the dean (the head of the local deanery), and only then should one consider speak to the bishop's office. The latter should be avoided if *at all* possible because (a) it will offend the priest if you go over his head, and (b) it will put the bishop or his office in the uncomfortable position of having to decide whether to speak to the priest about it. It is not as easy as many think for bishops to correct their priests.

If one does go to the bishop's office, it is important to provide specific documentation of the abuse. One is much more likely to get action if one can say, "On the following five dates the priest did this . . ." than if one says, "Recently my priest did something that was kind of funny during Mass."

In one's letter to the bishop's office, one should also cite the official text where the abuse is prohibited, and one should ask for a citation of another document, if there is one, that has changed the rule. Then look up that work, if any. One should always be willing to acknowledge that one has made a mistake and that there may be a more recent regulation, and one should look it up for oneself.

If it is necessary to speak to the bishop's office, one should attempt to be even more respectful, polite, and friendly than when one went to the priest. One should also explain that several members of the congregation (whom you name in the letter) have spoken to the priest, yet the abuse has not been corrected. One must also sign one's own name to the letter. Anonymous complaints do not tend to produce results, since in the eyes of the bishop's office, the person did not have the courage to sign his or her name and cannot be contacted to verify the information.

6. INVESTIGATE A MEDIATION OR CONCILIATION PROCESS

Besides taking the matter up the chain of authority, any available mediation or conciliation processes could be consulted if the situation is serious enough to warrant it. The *Code of Canon Law* states:

CANON 1733 §1

It is very desirable that whenever someone feels injured by a decree, there not be a contention between this person and the author of the decree but that care be taken by common counsel to find an equitable solution between them, perhaps through the use of wise persons in mediation and study so that the controversy may be avoided or solved by some suitable means.

Many dioceses have conciliation or mediation processes. It is a good idea to use them, not only because it might solve the problem at the local level, but also because it will contribute to your "paper trail." A paper trail will be needed if more formal procedures have to be employed, and it should include copies of all correspondence to and from Church officials you have contacted trying to get the abuse corrected, including one's local priest. If one wishes to pursue local conciliation or mediation, one should consult someone competent to give advice in how to handle it, such as a canon lawyer.

7. DETERMINE WHETHER FORMAL PROCEDURES ARE NEEDED

In most cases, the bishop's office is likely to be one's last resort in trying to get the abuse corrected. One could write to the Apostolic Pro-Nuncio in Washington, D.C., or to the Congregation for Divine Worship and the Discipline of the Sacraments. But one should not expect a visible result from doing so. Understand that both the pro-nuncio and the Holy See's congregations receive a great deal of mail and personal responses are not always possible.

> Most Rev. Agostino Cacciavillan
> Apostolic Nunciature
> 3339 Massachusetts Ave., N.W.
> Washington, DC 20008

Most Rev. Jorge Arturo Medina Estevez
Congregation for Divine Worship
   and the Discipline of the Sacraments
10 Piazza Pio XII 10
00193 Rome
ITALY

If one writes, one should use the opening salutation "Your Excellency:" instead of "Dear Archbishop," and the closing salutation "I have the honor to be, Your Excellency," instead of "Sincerely." One should also be aware that in almost all cases the correspondence will end up being handled by someone on staff and not by the person being addressed.

In order to have any real likelihood of obtaining action, one must take formal recourse to the appropriate authorities. This should only be done in the most serious of situations (e.g., something invalidating the Mass that is not being corrected). If things have progressed to this point, professional assistance is highly recommended. Consult a canon lawyer or the St. Joseph Foundation before deciding on or pursuing formal recourse.

Where to Go for More Help

Catholic Answers specializes in evangelization and apologetics. When we can, we try to help people with common liturgical questions, such as the ones discussed in this book. However, we do not specialize in answering detailed, technical questions on the liturgy, so it is worthwhile to mention the sources to which one *should* turn with detailed questions.

The Church's liturgical worship, although centered around the Mass, is also accomplished through the celebration of the sacraments, the Liturgy of the Hours, and various other rites. As a consequence, there is no one liturgical text that can serve as a source for the proper conduct for a particular act of public worship.

For the celebration of the Holy Sacrifice of the Mass, increasingly referred to as "the Liturgy" or "the Eucharist," there are two primary texts—the *Roman Missal* (Sacramentary) and the *Lectionary for Mass.*

The first source that a person should check is a copy of the Sacramentary or the Lectionary that is used at Mass. Copies of these may be ordered from Liturgical Press by calling 1-800-858-5450. These two works contain the official rubrics for Mass, which are sufficient to answer the great majority of questions. The rubrics must be followed unless one can produce a text approved by the Holy See that suspends a particular rubric in a particular circumstance. Within the Sacramentary, two prefaces that are particularly important are the *General Instruction of the Roman Missal* (GIRM) and its American appendix, which contains the adaptations of the liturgy authorized for the United States. (Sacramentaries prepared for use in other countries have their own national adaptations).

If the answer cannot be found in the GIRM, its appendix, or the rubrics, one should turn to a work summarizing the liturgy or to a standard collection of liturgical documents. One of the best general surveys of the liturgy is *Ceremonies of the Modern Roman Rite* by Msgr. Peter J. Elliott (San Francisco: Ignatius, 1995). Also very useful is *The Sacraments and Their Celebration* by Fr. Nicholas Halligan (New York: Alba House, 1986), which deals with all of the sacraments but has helpful information on the liturgies associated with the sacraments. Both of these works are obtainable from Catholic Answers.

Texts dealing with other forms of liturgy include:

The Rites of the Catholic Church (the *Roman Ritual* revised by decree of the Second Vatican Council; The Liturgical Press, 1990, vols. I, IA, and II) provides the rubrics for the administration of the sacraments, vows of religious persons, and the blessings of certain objects.

Book of Blessings (Liturgical Press, 1989) provides the norms and texts for the blessings of persons and groups on special occasions and that of objects and places.

Sunday Celebrations in the Absence of a Priest (Liturgical Press, 1997), provides the rubrics for communal worship under the leadership of a deacon or specially designated lay person.

Documents on the Liturgy: 1963–1979 (Liturgical Press, 1982). This work contains many, well-indexed liturgical materials covering the reign of Paul VI.

The translations used in the above books tend to be those prepared by the International Committee on English in the Liturgy (ICEL). When using these translations one must be watchful, because they contains a number of inaccurate renderings inspired by a dissident agenda (for example, they use the inaccurate translation "special ministers of the Eucharist" instead of "extraordinary ministers of the Eucharist"). All four of these works may be ordered from the number given above. Many liturgical documents can also be found on the World Wide Web.

If published resources are insufficient to find the answer, one may try calling the chancery of one's diocese and asking to speak to a canon lawyer. Though canon lawyers are not usually experts in liturgical law, they can often be helpful.

Two excellent organizations, both well worth your support, should also be mentioned as resources. The first exists to help

Catholics secure their ecclesial rights, including their liturgical rights, and the second exists to promote authentic liturgical reform in line with that envisioned by Vatican II. They are:

St. Joseph Foundation
11107 Wurzbach, Suite 601B
San Antonio, TX 78230-2570
210-697-0717 (voice)
210-699-9439 (fax)

Adoremus
P.O. Box 5858
Arlington, VA 22205
703-241-5858 (voice)
703-241-0068 (fax)

The U.S. Bishops' Guidelines for Receiving Communion

The following are the current Guidelines for Receiving Communion *that were approved by the U.S. bishops at their Fall 1996 meeting.*

For Catholics: As Catholics, we fully participate in the celebration of the Eucharist when we receive Communion. We are encouraged to receive Communion devoutly and frequently. In order to be properly disposed to receive Communion, participants should not be conscious of grave sin and normally should have fasted one hour. A person who is conscious of grave sin is not to receive the Body and Blood of the Lord without prior sacramental confession except for a grave reason where there is no opportunity for confession. In this case the person is to be mindful of the obligation to make an act of perfect contrition, including the intention of confessing as soon as possible (Canon 916). A frequent reception of the sacrament of penance is encouraged for all.

For our fellow Christians: We welcome our fellow Christians to this celebration of the Eucharist as our brothers and sisters. We pray that our common baptism and the action of the Holy Spirit in this Eucharist will draw us closer to one another and begin to dispel the sad divisions which separate us. We pray that these will lessen and finally disappear, in keeping with Christ's prayer for us "that they may all be one" (John 17:21).

Because Catholics believe that the celebration of the Eucharist is a sign of the reality of the oneness of faith, life, and worship, members of those churches with whom we are not yet fully united are ordinarily not admitted to Communion. Eucharistic sharing in exceptional circumstances by other Christians requires permission according to the directives of the diocesan bishop and the provisions of canon law (Canon 844 §4). Members of the Orthodox churches, the Assyrian Church of the East and the Polish National Catholic Church are urged to respect the discipline of their own churches. According to Roman Catholic discipline, the *Code of Canon Law* does not object to the reception of Communion by Christians of these churches (Canon 844 §3).

For those not receiving Communion: All who are not receiving Communion are encouraged to express in their hearts a prayerful desire for unity with the Lord Jesus and with one another.

For non-Christians: We also welcome to this celebration those who do not share our faith in Jesus Christ. While we cannot admit them to Communion, we ask them to offer their prayers for the peace and the unity of the human family.

The Holy See's
Translation Norms

The following are norms issued by the Holy See for translation of biblical texts. These prohibit the attempt to gender-revise texts in order to fit a modern social-political agenda and were sent to the U.S. bishops by Cardinal Joseph Ratzinger. They are presented here because of the comfort they will bring to the many people who are troubled by the gender-revisionist movement.

1. The Church must always seek to convey accurately in translation the texts she has inherited from the biblical, liturgical, and patristic tradition and instruct the faithful in their proper meaning.

2. The first principle with respect to biblical texts is that of fidelity, maximum possible fidelity to the words of the text. Biblical translations should be faithful to the original languages used by the human author in order to be understood by his intended reader. Every concept in the original text should be translated in its context. Above all, translations must be faithful to the sense of sacred Scripture understood as a unity and totality, which finds its center in Christ, the Son of God Incarnate (cf. DV [*Dei Verbum*] III and IV), as confessed in the creeds of the Church.

3. The translation of Scripture should faithfully reflect the Word of God in the original human languages. It must be listened to in its time-conditioned, at times even inelegant, mode

of human expression without "correction" or "improvement" in service of modern sensitivities.

a) In liturgical translations or readings where the text is very uncertain or in which the meaning is very much disputed, the translation should be made with due regard to the Neo-Vulgate.

b) If explanations are deemed to be pastorally necessary or appropriate, they should be given in editorial notes, commentaries, homilies, etc.

4/1. The natural gender of personae in the Bible, including the human author of various texts where evident, must not be changed, insofar as this is possible in the receptor language.

4/2. The grammatical gender of God, pagan deities, and angels and demons according to the original texts must not be changed, insofar as this is possible in the receptor language.

4/3. In fidelity to the inspired Word of God, the traditional biblical usage for naming the persons of the Trinity as Father, Son, and Holy Spirit is to be retained.

4/4. Similarly, in keeping with the Church's tradition, the feminine and neuter pronouns are not to be used to refer to the person of the Holy Spirit.

4/5. There shall be no systematic substitution of the masculine pronoun or possessive adjective to refer to God, in correspondence to the original text.

4/6. Kinship terms that are clearly gender-specific, as indicated by the context, should be respected in translation.

5. Grammatical number and person of the original texts ordinarily should be maintained.

6/1. Translation should strive to preserve the connotations as well as the denotations of words or expressions in the original and thus not preclude possible layers of meaning.

6/2. For example, where the New Testament or the Church's tradition have interpreted certain texts of the Old Testament in a Christological fashion, special care should be observed in the translation of these texts so that a Christological meaning is not precluded.

6/3. Thus, the word *man* in English should as a rule translate *adam* and *anthropos* since there is no one synonym which effectively conveys the play between the individual, the collectivity, and the unity of the human family so important, for example, to expression of Christian doctrine and anthropology.

Commonly Raised Issues

The following tables are based on some of the most commonly asked questions about liturgical practices. Not all of these practices are common—many of the prohibited ones are very uncommon—but people still inquire about them based on reports they have heard, even if they have never seen the practices themselves.

CHANGING WORDS	U.S. Status
Priest addresses people as "My brothers and sisters" and varies wording of admonitions to the congregation in the penitential rite and before the Lord's Prayer (pp. 78–80)—	Permitted
Priest changes the words of other, fixed prayers (pp. 23–26)—	Prohibited
Person doing a reading gender-revises Scripture to eliminate male references (pp. 87–89)—	Prohibited
A gender-revised or otherwise altered creed is used (pp. 96–97)—	Prohibited
Parish announcements are made during the concluding rites (p. 175)—	Permitted

INTRODUCTORY RITES	U.S. Status
Priest gives a general, sacramental absolution in the penitential rite (pp. 80–83) —	Prohibited
Penitential rite and "Lord have mercy" are omitted when rite of blessing and sprinkling is used (p. 83) —	Required

LITURGY OF THE WORD	U.S. Status
Lector uses a translation (such as the NRSV) that has not been approved by both the bishops *and* the Holy See for liturgical use in the United States (pp. 87–89) —	Prohibited
Homily is omitted on a Sunday or holy days of obligation (p. 94) —	Prohibited
Homily is omitted on weekdays (p. 94) —	Permitted
Someone other than a bishop, priest, or deacon gives the homily at Mass (pp. 94–96) —	Prohibited
Someone gives a talk in place of the homily on a Sunday or holy day of obligation (p. 94) —	Prohibited
The Creed is not said on a Sunday or solemnity (p. 97) —	Prohibited
Apostles' Creed is used in place of the Nicene Creed at a Mass for adults (p. 97) —	Prohibited

LITURGY OF THE EUCHARIST	*U.S. Status*
Priest does not wash his hands at the beginning of the liturgy of the Eucharist (pp. 106–108) —	Prohibited
Female altar servers are used (pp. 56–59) —	Permitted
A bell is not rung during the Eucharistic prayer (pp. 116–117) —	Permitted
People say parts of the Eucharistic prayer which are reserved to the priest, such as the *Per ipsum* ("Through him, with him, in him. . .") (p. 112) —	Prohibited
Priest uses an unapproved Eucharistic prayer or changes an approved one (pp. 113–115) —	Prohibited
Priest alters the words of consecration (pp. 118–119) —	Prohibited
Recipe for altar bread includes ingredients other than flour and water in the dough (except in an Eastern rite parish) (pp. 68–71) —	Prohibited
Communion Hosts which leave many crumbs are used (pp. 69–70) —	Prohibited
People hold hands during the Our Father (p. 161) —	Discouraged
Priest omits the exchange of an individual sign of peace (pp. 162–163) —	Permitted
Exchange of an individual sign of peace is relocated to another part of the Mass (p. 163) —	Prohibited

During the sign of peace the priest leaves the sanctu-
ary to shake hands with the congregation (p. 163)—   Prohibited

COMMUNION   *U. S. Status*

People at the altar receive Communion at the same
time as the priest (pp. 166–168)—   Prohibited

Extraordinary ministers of Holy Communion are
used excessively or unnecessarily (pp. 51–55)—   Prohibited

Minister or priest refuses a person the right to choose
whether to receive the Host on the tongue or in their
hands (except in case of Communion by intinction)
(pp. 154–155)—   Prohibited

Priest refuses extraordinary ministers and altar servers
the right to receive on the tongue (pp. 154–155)—   Prohibited

Communion under both kinds is given at all Masses
where it is permitted (p. 248)—   Preferred

The chalice is handed to the communicants (p.
153)—   Preferred

The communicants pick up the chalice from a table
(pp. 152–153)—   Prohibited

Communion is given to Protestants apart from the
special circumstances indicated in the *Code of Canon
Law* (pp. 137–141)—   Prohibited

Communion is given to Protestants at weddings and
funerals (p. 140)—   Prohibited

Children are not allowed to have First Confession before First Communion (pp. 144–152) —	Prohibited

PURIFICATION OF VESSELS	*U.S. Status*
Priest carefully and reverently collects and consumes or dissolves any particles from Hosts during the purification of the vessels (pp. 170–172) —	Required
Priest reverently dissolves any drops of the Precious Blood (pp. 170–171) —	Required
Unless it is being taken to the sick, all of the Precious Blood is consumed after Mass rather than reserved (pp. 173–174) —	Required
The Precious Blood is poured down a sink or sacrarium (p. 173) —	Prohibited
Vessels are purified by a deacon or another minister rather than by than the priest (pp. 170–172) —	Permitted
Vessels are purified after Mass (pp. 170–172) —	Permitted
Vessels are purified at a side table (pp. 170–172) —	Preferred

LITURGICAL ARTICLES AND FURNISHINGS	*U.S. Status*
Eucharistic vessels are made of materials other than metal (pp. 189–191) —	Permitted
Chalice is made of an absorbent material, such as unglazed clay, or an ungilded and corrosion-prone material, such as silver (p. 190) —	Prohibited

Baskets are used to hold consecrated Hosts (p. 190)—	Prohibited
The altar is used exclusively for divine worship (p. 187)—	Required
There is a cross on or near the altar during Mass (pp. 187–189)—	Required
The altar cross has an image of the crucified Christ on it (pp. 188–189)—	Preferred
Tabernacle is located on the central axis of the nave (pp. 191–192)—	Permitted
Tabernacle is located in a hard-to-find, out-of-the-way chapel (p. 192)—	Prohibited
A parish has no kneelers or has its kneelers taken out (pp. 206–207)—	Discouraged
There are no images of the saints in the church (pp. 181–182)—	Prohibited

POSTURES AND ACTIONS	*U.S. Status*
People genuflect when passing in front of the Eucharist, whether in the tabernacle or publicly exposed (pp. 207–208)—	Required
Neither a genuflection nor a deep bow is made by those carrying articles in the entrance procession (p. 208)—	Preferred

People kneel after the end of the *Sanctus* and remain kneeling through the consecration until after the Great Amen (pp. 204–206)—	Required
People remain standing during the consecration due to the fact that there are no kneelers (pp. 206–207)—	Prohibited
People stand around the altar holding hands during the consecration (pp. 203–204)—	Prohibited
People assume any posture that is helpful to them —standing, sitting, or kneeling—as soon as they return from Communion (p. 206)—	Permitted
People imitate gestures made by the priest that are appropriate to his role (pp. 202, 211)—	Prohibited
Dancing of any kind is performed during a liturgical service (pp. 211–214)—	Prohibited
Ministers below the rank of deacon wear albs, including lectors, altar servers, and extraordinary ministers of Holy Communion (p. 199)—	Permitted

Seasonal Practices

	U. S. Status
Blue is used as a liturgical color in Advent or Lent (p. 201)—	Prohibited
Crosses are veiled before the close of the Mass of the Lord's Supper on Holy Thursday (p. 246)—	Prohibited
Women have feet washed on Holy Thursday (p. 44)—	Prohibited

Holy water fonts are refilled with water blessed at
Easter Vigil (p. 179)—   Required

Index

Addenda

CHURCH'S LITURGICAL DOCUMENTS

The following question and answer regarding the non-authoritative status of *Environment and Art in Catholic Worship* (EACW) are given on the National Conference of Catholic Bishops' web site:

> *What is the authority of the document* Environment and Art in Catholic Worship?
>
> *Environment and Art in Catholic Worship* is a 1978 statement of the Bishops' Committee on the Liturgy. The purpose of the document is to provide principles for those involved in preparing liturgical space. The committee statement received the approval of the Administrative Committee in keeping with Conference policy. Because the document was not proposed as a statement of the whole conference of Bishops, the full body of bishops was never asked to consider it.
>
> *Environment and Art in Catholic Worship* does not have the force of law in and of itself. It is not particular law for the dioceses of the United States of America, but a commentary on that law by the Committee for the Liturgy. However, it does quote several documents of the Apostolic See and in that sense it has the force of the documents it quotes in the areas where those documents legislate.
>
> The Bishops' Committee on the Liturgy has appointed a task group to revisit *Environment and Art in Catholic Worship*. The Committee on the Liturgy intends to submit the revised edition of this document as a statement of the Conference of Bishops. It is therefore anticipated that the revised

document will be considered by the full body of Bishops. [www.nccbuscc.org/liturgy/q&a/environment/environment.htm]

The statement that EACW "does quote several documents of the Apostolic See and in that sense it has the force of the documents it quotes in the areas where those documents legislate" is true of any work quoting authoritative documents (this book included). EACW still does not have any legislative authority of its own.

Preparation for Mass

Veiling of Crosses and Images. Though episcopal conferences are authorized to permit the veiling of crosses and images on the Saturday before the fifth Sunday of Lent (see p. 64), the U.S. bishops' conference has not done so. Consequently, it is not permitted in the United States. The NCCB's *Committee on Liturgy Newsletter* states:

> The National Conference of Catholic Bishops has never voted to continue the practice of covering crosses and images and so the practice, in accord with the rubric of the *Sacramentary*, has not been permissible for the past twenty-five years. Individual parishes are not free to reinstate the practice on their own [NCCB, *Committee on Liturgy Newsletter* (April 1995) 31:14].

However, in accordance with *Paschales Solemnitatis*, crosses are still veiled following the Mass of the Lord's Supper on Holy Thursday (see p. 65). This matter was not left to the discretion of the national conference.

Liturgy of the Word

New Lectionary. The first volume of a two-volume lectionary based largely on the *Revised New American Bible* (see p. 89) has been approved for use in the U.S. beginning with Advent, 1998. As of this writing, the second volume has not yet received approval for use at Mass. It is anticipated that, once the second volume is approved, the completed lectionary will be the only one permitted for use at Mass in the United States. Until then, the other, already approved lectionaries may still be used (see pp. 87–88). On June 19, 1998, Bishop Anthony M. Pilla, President of the NCCB, issued a decree that stated, in part:

> The first volume of the Lectionary for Mass was canonically approved for use by the National Conference of Catholic Bishops on June 20, 1992 and was subsequently confirmed by the Apostolic See by decree of the Congregation for Divine Worship and the Discipline of the Sacraments on October 6, 1997 (Prot. 1667/97/L).
>
> On the First Sunday of Advent, November 29, 1998, the first volume of the Lectionary for Mass may be used in the liturgy. Upon promulgation of the second volume of the Lectionary for Mass a date for mandatory use will be established [NCCB, *Committee on Liturgy Newsletter*, June 1998].

COMMUNION RITE

Preference for Consumption of Hosts. It is preferred that the faithful receive Hosts consecrated at the same Mass they are attending. Of course, this is not always possible, which is part of the reason for the reservation of Hosts in a Tabernacle. It is necessary to regularly consume the Hosts kept in the Tabernacle to prevent the species from going stale and corrupting (CDW, *Holy Communion and Worship of the Eucharist outside Mass* [June 21, 1973] 7 [DOL 2199]). Nevertheless, to the extent possible, it is preferred that the faithful receive Hosts consecrated at the Mass they are attending. It is also preferred that Communion under both kinds be given when it is permitted. The rubrics in the Sacramentary state:

> It is important that the faithful should receive the Body of the Lord in Hosts consecrated at the same Mass and should share the cup when it is permitted. Communion is thus a clearer sign of sharing in the sacrifice which is actually taking place [*Sacramentary* (1985 ed.), 415].

Preference for Communion under Both Kinds. The preference, expressed in the preceding quotation from the Sacramentary, that the laity receive Communion under both kinds when it is offered is also expressed in the U.S. bishops' document, *This Holy and Living Sacrifice*:

> Communion under both kinds is to be desired in all celebrations of the Mass, although this is not possible in all cases [HLS 19].

At the discretion of the local ordinary, Communion under both kinds is permitted at all Sunday and weekday Masses (see p. 158), with the following exceptions:

> a. at Masses celebrated in the open with a great number of communicants (e.g., in a stadium);
> b. at other Masses where the number of communicants is so great as to make it difficult for Communion under both kinds to be given in an orderly and reverent way (e.g., Masses celebrated in a civic square or building that would involve the carrying of the sacred species up and down a number of steps);
> c. at Masses where the assembled congregation is of such a diverse nature that it is difficult to ascertain whether those present have been sufficiently instructed about receiving Communion under both kinds;
> d. when circumstances do not permit the assurance that due reverence can be maintained towards the consecrated wine both during and after the celebration (cf. *Inaestimabile Donum*, 13–14) [HLS 22].